THE COLOR HUMAN

A Psychohistory of Self and Other, Race and Class and the Complexion of Things

Naomi Rucker, Ph.D. and Karen Lombardi, Ph.D.

The Color Human:
A Psychohistory of Self and Other, Race and Class, and the Complexion of Things
Copyright © 2023 by Naomi Rucker, Ph.D. and Karen Lombardi, Ph.D.
All rights reserved.

No part of this book may be used or reproduced in any manner whatsoever without written permission, except in the case of brief quotations embodied in critical articles and reviews. For more information, e-mail all inquiries to info@mindstirmedia.com.

Published by Mindstir Media, LLC
45 Lafayette Rd | Suite 181| North Hampton, NH 03862 | USA
1.800.767.0531 | www.mindstirmedia.com

Printed in the United States of America
ISBN-13: 978-1-960142-56-6

DEDICATION
Naomi Rucker

To my dear lifelong friends, Rachel Cohen, Cathy Mermelstein, and Cynthia (Thea) Turner with whom I have shared warm friendship and laughter, and who have been stalwart sources of support, affection, and comfort for decades. They may learn new things about me from this book, but they all know me well. To Thea especially, I will miss you always.

And to my children and grandson, Philip, Clara, and Lee, who have been the best parts of my life. I am inordinately proud of all of you! My wish that you know my Self-before-you was the genesis of this book…it is still my wish, so I hope that you will read it!

ACKNOWLEDGEMENTS
Naomi Rucker

I first want to acknowledge my parents, Bunny and Helen Rucker, for their tireless efforts to do their very best for me out of love, regardless of their so-very-human flaws and failings. I thank them lovingly for all that they did give, and I forgive them lovingly for all that they could not. I also admire their courage, their vision, their convictions, and their humanistic values and principles. These have guided me well. My parents also taught me to enjoy language and reading, to develop vocabulary, and to write well, a skill that I think I have passed along to my children. These pleasures have been invaluable to me.

I am full of gratitude for my beloved Nanny, Clara Emmeline Rose Muenich, who nurtured, loved, and strove to protect me every moment of my childhood and whom I have loved specially. She was a figure of grace in my childhood home. I hope that I have taken in some of my family's best qualities along with all the rest. Connected to Nanny is Tassie, initially Nanny's dog who became our family pet through her sixteen years, and whom I also loved specially. Together they were my safe haven in childhood. Tassie's spirit has been present in my affinity for dogs and in my bonds with all the fur-children who have crossed my path. She should not be overlooked just because she was only partly human!

I am grateful to my friend, Alitta Kullman, an author and analyst in her own right, for nudging me to move this project from a note to my children to a book. I thank her warmly for her guidance and for her contribution to the title. Pam Lloyd, with whom I share a love of dogs, horses, and walking in the woods, is much appreciated for her encouragement and generous support. I also acknowledge Karen Estep for her love and support of my daughter and their son, my grandson Lee, and I do so with admiration for her many personal talents. She enhances our family all the time.

Both of my analysts, who I will not name, have earned much appreciation for their insights, their affection, and their years of engagement with me. I must thank my first analyst posthumously, but hopefully my second analyst will read my words. For better or worse, but generally a good bit better, our relationships have been critical to whom I have become and to the existence of *The Color Human*.

Although I dedicate this book to three very special friends, I also wish to mention a number of other people whose closeness and friendship over many years have mattered greatly to me at various points in my adult life. I have ongoing connections with all of them now. In no particular order, they are: Elyse Lee, Rob Brager, Anna Lee, Robin Shafran, Beth Levine, Beth Green, Patrice Butterfield, Elizabeth Slater, Douglas Bernon, Debbie Goldman, Vivian Beckford, Claude and Louis Boyle, Peter Brody, Ellen Lea, Brenda Goodhart, Sherry McCumber. And Michael Levy, who occupies a particular niche among my personal relationships, deserves a very fond nod.

Of course, I most warmly recognize Karen Lombardi, who enthusiastically agreed to work with me on this book, for the richness and depth that she has brought to it. Her ability to peel away layers and "see" all that is there is a marvel. Karen and I are closing our careers with a lot to say as both lasting friends and colleagues. She is the person in my life who most well appreciates the bittersweetness of being human, as I do. As contemporary psychology continues the disheartening enthrallment with empiricism and "science" that is draining the soul from the study of the mind, I like to think that Karen and I have once again amplified the voice of the Unconscious. We know in our hearts and minds that the Unconscious may be ignored, but it cannot be silenced. It echoes endlessly in and around us, always.

Karen Lombardi

When Naomi invited me to collaborate on what has become this book, I was both delighted and challenged. I was invited to comment on her memoir and the individual and cultural influences, both conscious and implicitly unconscious, surrounding and affecting her. In this process, I was challenged to examine my own life and the ways our two lives intersected, both materially and psychically. Naomi and I have collaborated before, having co-authored professional journal articles as well as a book entitled *Subject Relations: Unconscious Experience in Relational Psychoanalysis*. We found ourselves to be natural collaborators, as our interests, our thoughts, and our experiences seem to intersect, sometimes in uncanny ways. As is usual in our relationships with fellow human beings, we are aware of our similarities while below our awareness, on an unconscious level, deeper connections exist. Working together on this book has revealed some of those unconscious psychic connections that we share. These unconscious connections are part of the human condition, a process that is common to all of us in our relationships with others. I am grateful to her for the invitation to engage in this process.

I could not have written the words in this book, nor any of the articles and presentations I have made during my career, without the inspiration of my students. In my many years as a professor teaching in a doctoral program in clinical psychology, I have had the pleasure of training talented, bright, creative psychologists-to-be, many of whom have become friends and colleagues. I am grateful to them for enlivened discussions, for deepening my thinking, and for keeping me young.

Similarly, I could not have contributed to this book without the influence of those who have trained me, including my revered teachers Dr. Gilbert Trachtman, Dr. Lawrence Balter, and especially to Dr. Joseph Newirth, who has been my mentor, colleague, and friend. Without Joe, I would not have been the psychologist and psychoanalyst I am today.

My friends and colleagues, with whom I share an intellectual and personal life, deserve special mention. I have known my dear friend Dr. Eva Lapidos since our years in graduate school together. Throughout the years we have found ourselves in each other, especially through our love of reading and our concern for the state of things. To Dr. Carl Paris, a multitalented former professional dancer and current professor of Africana Studies, who has shared his writings with me as I have with him, as well as sharing our concern for life in these United States. Also to my colleagues, Dr. Michael O'Loughlin and Dr. Kirkland Vaughans, who remain my comrades-in-arms as our doctoral program has gone through many changes over the years.

To my daughter, Chloe, who has been the light of my life since we first gazed into each other's eyes, and to my mother, who was a very special loving

Nana to Chloe. Chloe, a talented visual artist with a poetic soul, recently has chosen the path of psychoanalysis herself. It is an honor to be her mother.

Finally, I return to my relationship with Naomi. I find myself in her, and my hope is that you, reader, will recognize parts of yourself in the process of reading this book.

From both of us,

We extend warm thanks to the editors, designers, and staff from Manhattan Book Group who worked with us on *The Color Human*. It is a pleasure to have made this book a reality! We could not have navigated the editorial work without the expert computer assistance of Chloe Lombardi Civin. Without her, this volume would never have seen its final form. And to the people at Abraham Lincoln Brigade Archives (ALBA) for their specific effort to find a photo that I wished to include here, and for their daily efforts to preserve a truly important, but often disregarded, piece of American history. We also thank Dr. Elizabeth Slater, Peter Carroll, Dr. Kirkland Vaughans for their openness to reading and reviewing our manuscript, and for their interest, time, and attention spent doing so. It takes a village….!

"Il reste toujours quelque chose de l'enfance, toujours"
(Marguerite Duras 1914-1996)

PREFACE

The Color Human began as a memoir, but in the end the depth of the book rendered the term "memoir" insufficient. It is not a recitation of selected life events as consciously experienced, as in a memoir or autobiography, but a sojourn through the evolution of a human psyche that emphasizes unconscious themes, processes, and connections in the creation of an individual. The emphasis on the primacy of unconscious life, and the rich rendition of emotional experience, differentiate this book as a psychohistory from the genre of memoir.

In *The Color Human*, we place a personal life experience and emotional history in the social, cultural, political milieux that surrounded it and within the context of the familial psychological patterns, dynamics, and trauma that have shaded this particular life. The synthesis of personal and external factors creates a psychological and psychocultural complexion that each individual contributes to his or her psychological lineage — an emotional coloring that is both born from and gives birth to the continuing histories of all those with whom he or she forms emotional bonds. The word "complexion" is chosen for this description because it has a particular meaning in this specific life story, but another word such as "resonance" would also convey the reverberations of psychological and emotional elements through generations. These reverberations offer us our humanity by making each of us human as one of a collective species, and human as a singular being.

Our book is divided into two sections: the psychohistory, written by Dr. Rucker about her life as she lived and felt it, and the sociocultural/political/psychoanalytic commentary that follows, written by Dr. Lombardi. The sections are neither purely separate nor mutually exclusive, but each is dominated by the thought process and writing from one of us, respectively. The ideas exist apart from the story, and the story exists apart from the ideas, but their synergy creates dimensions that illustrate something new. The life experiences reported here are Dr. Rucker's, but Dr. Lombardi's integration of her story with broader perspectives reflects the interplay between individual experience and its interpersonal and cultural surrounds.

The Color Human also represents the psychological lineage of our bond with each other over our almost forty-year personal and professional affiliation. Our relationship began with a mutual intellectual affinity, became a lasting friendship, and transformed into a deep connection of like-minds as we worked and shared together over the years. We have embodied many incarnations of Self, Other, Self-in-Other, Other-in-Self over the years, often thinking in tandem. Writing this book together at the end of both of our professional lives caps multiple joint endeavors that have emerged from our conscious and unconscious connections, from papers to presentations to an earlier book on psychoanalytic theory and clinical process entitled *Subject Relations: Unconscious Experience and Relational Psychoanalysis (1998)*. As the reader will come to appreciate in the reference to a simile embedded in Dr. Rucker's narrative, we have come to intuit each other's unspoken thoughts, sometimes as if we were one mind with two heads.

As the reader may also notice, we do not ascribe to the dominance of neurology as fundamental to understanding human experience or the human mind. In this we differ greatly from the tenor of the times in virtually all mental health fields, save psychoanalysis. Neurology, biology, genetics now preoccupy the attention of researchers, theorists, clinicians at the exclusion of other modes of studying human psychology. These approaches, which emphasize difference over similarity, serve the scientific experimental model well, while compromising an appreciation of the richness of the human spirit.

The emphasis on genetics focuses on innate differences, inborn and immutable, without regard to the psychic relational processes through which genetics unfold and in which all humans engage. As all humans share 99.6% of our genetic material, and only 0.4% distinguishes us as individuals (National Institute of General Medical Sciences), the vast majority of humanity is shared. Differences among us are minor in comparison to our commonalities. In focusing on the physiological aspects of human beings at the expense of the psychical, psychologists have attended to trees (the 0.4%), while ignoring the forest (the 99.6%).

For example, one's basic mood state, his or her emotional "set point," as it is sometimes called, need not be understood as founded in genetics or neurology, as it usually is described. Rather, it can be explained as the consequence of unconscious affects exchanged during the last months of pregnancy and the early months of life between a fetus and tiny infant with his or her primary caregivers, especially the biological/psychological mother. It is facile to default to a genetic explication when we have no direct measurable information about these earliest interactions, but it is not necessarily accurate. What is inborn is not necessarily genetic; what is present at birth is not necessarily biological. The quality of the unconscious, psychical interactions that form mood or other emotional features may be individual, but their presence before and after birth is universal among humans.

With a nod to Robert Frost's famous poetic metaphor about two roads that diverged in a wood, we, the authors of this book, have chosen the road less traveled. We do not walk along the scientific path that controls, measures, quantifies conscious aspects of human experience, addressing difference and distinction within the human collective. Rather, we embrace the depth, beauty, and meaning that valuing the power and ubiquity of the unconscious mind, common to all people, brings to our understanding of human personhood, the human condition, and human kinship. This psychohistory draws attention to the complexity of unconscious relational processes in the development of one individual psyche, while it enlightens and informs our cognizance of relational patterns in all people and relationships.

Here, in *The Color Human,* we address the personal and the collective, the internal and the external, and the conscious manifestations of things unconsciously processed. This book is not intended to be primarily a psychoanalytic work for psychoanalytic readers but rather an illumination of psychological qualities, both collectively human and individually expressed, that can be appreciated by all. Nonetheless, we hope to bridge gaps between dichotomies inherent in the human condition through details of one psychic life and the richness of psychoanalytic formulations. We both are, after all, by nature and nurture, psychoanalysts.

So, with this framework established, we turn to Dr. Rucker's opening thoughts on her autobiographical narrative. The peregrination through the first half of her life that unfolds between the covers of this book, followed by Dr. Lombardi's enlightening reflections and associations, will then begin.

NR and KL
January 2023

INTRODUCTION TO PART ONE
Naomi Rucker, Ph.D.

The embryonic beginning of *The Color Human* lies in my desire to tell the tale of my life for my grown children and grandson, who seem at this point in their lives not especially interested or too young to know that he might be interested. I anticipate that there might come a time when they would want to know things about me, but alas the telling will no longer be possible. This book has grown, as embryos do, in leaps and bounds, from a small recitation of my life written as a memoir to a much larger exploration of what has made me, me. It also has come to involve my dear friend, colleague, and professional alter-ego, Karen Lombardi, who enriches my thoughts and ideas now as she has done for decades. Although much of our lives have been separate, our minds have not, a notion that will become clear as you read along. Although the life that *The Color Human* explores is mine alone, we are a team in the endeavor to do so.

This psychohistory blends many thoughts and recollections about my life, my family, and the culture around us that have gathered in my conscious and unconscious minds over decades. It calls forth material from my earliest life through my early 30s in detailed, honest, and highly personal ways, but it does not "tell all." It does not omit essential elements of my early life, but, at points in my writing, I chose to be cautiously selective. While reading, it also is important to keep in mind the impact of the "white bread" Zeitgeist in the United States during the 1950s-60s that frames much of this story. The press for conventionality, conformity, uniformity, and the shunning of ethnic and other cultural differences that dominated in those decades is the antithesis of the call for diversity that has exploded in more recent times. The notion of diversity did not exist then as it does now, and the powerful enforcement of Othering and the suppression of issues of race and class that did exist exerted pressure on my parents, my family, myself (my Self). Lastly, the story that I tell does not continue into my middle and later adulthood, except in a cursory fashion that may be frustrating to some readers. I hope that you, who are frustrated, have questions, wish to know more, or to hear "how it all ends" will understand my choice to keep some things private.

Delving into my ancient past is sort-of comfortable, but detailing my more recent past feels too intrusive and exposing regarding both myself and others. My childhood family is long deceased, but the loved ones in my current life are not. I choose not to subject them to the analytic scrutiny that is the essence of this book, nor to expose personal details about them to the public eye. Hopefully, you will understand as you read about my psyche and my life that my needs for self-protection have a long and deep history. I have relinquished them willingly to share my inner world here; being "seen" is a personal impetus for self-expression that co-exists, and sometimes conflicts, with my needs for privacy. Yet, as in a play, when enough has been said, the curtain must come down, the audience must go home, and the actors must retire. The story of a play, as with this writing, continues in the thoughts and fantasies of those who were touched by it.

My life, as is true perhaps of all lives, has been a conglomeration of elements that sometimes fit together smoothly, but often connect awkwardly and jarringly. Yet, I think that the particular configuration of elements and their juxtaposition within my family and my experiences were more awkward and jarring than often is the case. However, this may not be true. This idea may be an expression of the narcissistic streak that is present in anyone who writes a memoir of any kind; a memoir or autobiography or psychohistory is a rather narcissistic project. Nonetheless, as I face my 70s, I will allow myself this indulgence. You, the reader, may agree that my experiences are "more" than usual; you may feel very emotionally separate from me and aligned with others. Or, to some extent, you may find yourself (and your Self) here in this book, which is my wish. In either case, I hope that my writing will convey, at the very least, some of that awkward, jarring feeling; it is one that I carry with me all the time.

This psychohistory draws upon an appreciation of connections and disconnections between similarity and difference, personal and cultural histories, conscious and unconscious aspects of living, and shades of experience and meaning that comprise humanity. It expresses many of my Selves and those of the Others who were most essential in my life. My Self as a daughter, a granddaughter, a baby, child, adolescent, young adult, a mother, a psychoanalyst stands beside the Selves of my parents, grandmother, friends, classmates who were Others to me. It is also, perhaps, an unconscious/semi-conscious attempt to gather together these elements of Selves; to collect myself by collecting my Selves; to shape recollections from re-collections.

Yet, I do recognize that Self is in Other, and that Other is in Self, that absolute distinctions between Self and Other, as between Race and Class, are an artifice and an illusion. Themes of race and class were chosen for particular exploration because they overshadowed other matters in the nature of my family, my family history, my connections and disconnections with others and with the culture around me. Ultimately, they were critical in molding the child who I was and the adult who I became.

My father dominates much of my childhood tale, as his forceful personality dominated my childhood home. My mother, however, was the unflinching backbone of the household, quietly and tenaciously keeping things straight. Her unassuming nature and her subdued role in this psychohistory should not distract from her profound and complex role in my outer and inner lives. My maternal grandmother was the gentle, steady, healing presence that offered all of us soft landings under trying circumstances. Notwithstanding painful vicissitudes of living, and damage done along the way, when all was said and done, we were bonded, held together as a family, and saw it through. The devil was in the details.

We, the authors, place psychoanalytic theory and sociocultural observation largely in Part Two of this book, in favor of a more accessible and uninterrupted rendition of personal remembrances and experiences. Nonetheless, as the sociocultural milieux of my childhood and early adulthood, which include psychoanalysis, are a large part of my Self, they cannot be just an Other, relegated to the back. They are here, present in my interpretation of personal history and events, and in the occasional fortuitous comment, before they come forth in Dr. Lombardi's commentary. She is the best person to discuss and interpret my life experience, because she has often been inside my head! And because I trust her with my most sensitive and private feelings. Additionally, I admire her excellent grasp of theory, which is much broader than mine. She has been a model for my own psychoanalytic thinking, and we write and work together well. *The Color Human* would not be at all the book it is without her thoughts, feelings, and insights.

The experiences, memories, reflections that are essential to my contribution to this book largely are the culmination of many years of psychoanalytic study and my own psychoanalyses. I entered psychoanalysis twice at two separate points in my life, first as a young clinical psychology graduate student in my early twenties in New York City, and again in my mid-thirties as a mother and practicing psychoanalyst in Southern California. Ultimately, I had fifteen years of formal psychoanalysis three to five days a week. There is such a thing as "too much psychoanalysis," and fifteen years qualifies. Among the ramifications of lengthy psychoanalysis is the loss of denial and repression, the loss of the ability to "not know or un-know" painful things, and sometimes just having too many feelings. At the same time that psychoanalysis tickles the intellect and relieves distress, it is painful in its own right; there is no gain without some pain. The rewards are inwardly felt but not always readily seen. As has been the case often in my life, others may not notice.

For me, this book is an important symbol and forum for the emotions, energy, time, and money that I invested through my psychoanalyses, an investment that brought rich private rewards but also frustration and disappointment. Writing this psychohistory allows me to honor myself openly for my years spent trying to understand and alleviate my personal hurt, and for the insight and awareness that I have internalized in the process. My emotional life has become easier with attention and time, even though there has been no "magic." I still carry my share of emotional struggles and pain, but I absolutely have developed understandings of myself, my family, the course of my life, and the dynamics of people and their relationships that I never would have absorbed without my many years of "lying on the couch." The kernel of *The Color Human* as an idea, and its birth later as the book that you are reading, must, however, be credited to the arrival of a first grandchild, which led me to consider seriously the legacy that I would leave for him.

My writing is a bit circuitous, because that is how my experiences feel and present themselves to me. My thoughts are not quite linear, they meander, but they all reach a center from different angles. I have tried to impose some structure here for the sake of better comprehension, but the free associative quality of my thinking, bred from my many years of psychoanalysis, seeps through nonetheless. That is not a bad thing; it is a valued part of my psychological and psychoanalytic Self. My wish is that you, the reader, will wander with me. Hopefully this journey, in both substance and form, will capture the intricate and tangled weave of Selves and Others, Race and Class, and the multiple and layered interpretations of events that lend us our human complexion.

PART ONE

REVISITING REMEMBRANCES

PROLOGUE

To understand my history well, the reader must grasp the background dynamics of my family and certain features of my early childhood psyche. I will first introduce myself as a very young girl through scenes from my innermost life. One might think that these memories and dreams were experienced by four different children. But they were not. They represent four different motifs in my psychic life. The parts of myself, the Selves expressed in these images, have not always been integrated, but they all have co-existed. These memory and dream images are my earliest organized recollections of my own internal life. Any that came before are amorphous and not amenable to words.

You, the reader, are free to form your own interpretations of these scenes, if you wish. This should be easier after reading the narrative, but your first impressions before doing so might surprise you. The bulk of my life history will follow, beginning with the story of my parents and their relationship—the seeds of my beginning.

A hint:
Early memories and dreams capture the Past as Prologue. They entwine conscious memory with unconscious experience, intermingling external and internal realities, as do psychohistories, memoirs, autobiographies. The "facts" in dreams and early memories may not always be completely accurate, but the affective experiences that they convey express and form a lasting personal truth. Early memories, especially, are a retrospective view of the psychic life that we were living at the time, and also a coup d'œil for the life that then was ahead of us, the one still to be created. I hope that these images from my very

young self will stay with you, the reader, as you read this portrayal of my life. They are a guide to what is to come.

Two memories from toddlerhood - around age two:

1. Being pushed in a stroller on a warm, sunny day. Looking down at my white leather baby shoes against the metal-plated footrest of the stroller. Muted tones of silver, white, and sky blue. Cool and pretty. Feeling calm and contented.
2. Sitting in high chair with my mother next to me. I'm eating a jelly doughnut. My favorite! And I want all of it! My mother has given me a piece, but she puts the rest of the doughnut on top of the refrigerator out of my reach. I stand up in my high chair angrily, reaching for the doughnut. *If you won't give it to me, I will get it myself!* A palette of primary colors, red, blue, yellow. Full of energy, emotion, rage.

Two early-childhood dreams:

1. A nightmare at age four: Coming down on a roller coaster, going too fast. The roller coaster is tall, black with white rails, surrounded by a night sky dotted with lights. There are no people. Will my father be able to catch me at the bottom?? Frightened.
2. Repetitive dream element from age four to about twelve, and again briefly at twenty-four: There is a person, a figure of a young child or toddler, who clearly looks like me in a photo of myself at that age. Short wavy hair, round face, my complexion, dressed in blue overalls. The child is not clearly male, nor female, and stands silently—still, watchful, aloof, no clear emotion or facial expression. In the actual photo, I am washing my father's ears with a washcloth while he is in the bathtub. I am about two, wearing blue overalls. He is smiling…we are having fun. In my dreams, something is happening that is going to be bad, dangerous, frightening, but it does not quite materialize. I look around for this figure, because it is familiar and non-threatening, hoping it will help me, but it is nowhere to be seen. It is never there when I need it. Neutral colors, blue overalls always stand out.

1
ORIGINS

Even after living in Southern California and southeastern Georgia for most of my adult life, the Borough of Manhattan in New York City during the mid-1950s holds the heart of my personality, the beginning of myself. It is the place where my parents met and married, where I was born, and where I lived as a young child. My early memories are there, capturing the charm and delight of those early years but also wisps of the sadness that became a cloud around me as time passed and life evolved. For a brief time, my family, which included my parents, myself, and my maternal grandmother, lived in projects in the Bronx. My parents were interracially married, a rare marriage in those years—one that was still illegal in the South and highly controversial in the North, especially in 1943 when they were wed. Their union drew condemnation, contempt, and occasions of violence outside of their own family and small social circle. Neither originally were New Yorkers, but they were drawn to each other for tangled reasons in New York City.

My father, nicknamed Bunny, was of mixed black, white, and Native American heritage. His Cherokee ancestors were among those who fled to the South Carolina hills to escape the forced relocation to Oklahoma in the infamous Trail of Tears. Both of my paternal grandparents, however, attended black colleges in the South. My grandmother studied at Tuskegee and my father at Harpur College in Georgia, which was burned down repeatedly by the Klu Klux Klan and rebuilt repeatedly by its students.

Bunny was the third of twelve children in a poor black family that fled the South to settle in Ohio in 1912. The eldest child, a boy, died before my father was born. Fleeing was necessary because my grandfather assaulted a white overseer with a rock after the overseer made a threatening and disparaging remark about his pregnant wife. My father was born along the way, in Virginia, and was left with relatives for a few years while the rest of the family continued their hurried journey to safety. He did not have a birth certificate because black babies at that time were not issued birth certificate; they were not considered fully as people. My father with his grandmother joined his family later in Ohio, apparently in good health, but there is no information on the quality of care that he received in his first home. This episode in my family history is rather shrouded in mystery. My father did not talk about it, and the details seem to have been lost over time.

My father did discuss his parents' mixed-race heritage to emphasize the motley complexion of our family. My paternal grandmother was the offspring of a white man and a Cherokee Indian, and my paternal grandfather was the offspring of a white man (probably a slave owner or the like) and a black woman. The Rucker children in my father's generation, his siblings, spanned the spectrum of skin color, from very dark to "near-white," as the phrase goes. Genetically, my father was likely more white than black, but no one would have ever considered that to be the case. As a cousin of mine quipped at a family reunion: "If it hadn't been for Joseph Rucker (my paternal grandfather), we would all be white!"

Bunny was a brown-skinned man of average height with a big, warm smile. When he hugged you, you felt that all was safe with him in your world. He had deep thoughts and feelings and a capacity for passion. As a young man, my father was handsome and fit, even though he had become bald after having spinal meningitis at age twenty. His father became a Christian pastor who taught himself about Judaism and learned Hebrew. His mother worked hard to rear their children with little money and faced repeated criticism and judgement from Social Services about their growing family. During much of his childhood, my father lived in Ohio with an aunt as the children in the family eventually were dispersed among relatives. As the family grew, it became harder to provide for everyone. In contrast to its rarity among whites, the practice of sending children to live with relatives was not uncommon among black families. Perhaps this finds roots in slavery when children were taken from parents, and adults took care of other slaves' children, maybe with the hope that others would do the same with their lost children. The concept of "family," by necessity, was elastic.

Aunt Minnie, who raised my father, had extremely light skin and appeared white, and she lived alone in the white section of town. Unlike his siblings who shared living situations, my father was the only child living in this home, had more material possessions, and was able to go to "white schools." Although he developed close ties with his brothers and sisters, there was always a thread of resentment and envy among them. His large family provided me with many aunts, uncles, and cousins, but most of them lived in Ohio, and as I was born in my parents' middle-age, my first cousins were much older than me, and my second cousins were much younger. I did know them and had relationships with a few of them, but none were close childhood companions. I imagine that my father's early exposure to both his almost-white aunt and to white schools predisposed him to marry a white woman and move among the white, educated populace—within the dominant caste in American society as Isabel Wilkerson, in her recent book, *Caste*, describes.

I was named after my father's favorite sister, Naomi, and his late mother, Gabrella (my middle name). My mother's life history had no place in my name. Noni, as my aunt was called, was light-skinned, and my mother physically resembled her, although Noni's raucous temperament was antithetical to my mother's soft nature. My father's attraction to my mother likely was based partly on similarities in the features and fair complexions of her and his sister, although Noni's temperament was more similar to that of my father. Noni and my father resonated with each other psychologically, and they always had a special, though sometimes rancorous, bond. They were Self-in-Others to one another. My mother's gentleness provided balance and stability for my father's emotional intensity and volatility, akin to Noni's, while her likeness to Noni kept Noni psychically close for my father. My mother was just Other enough, separate and different but also familiar, not as alien as their racial and class differences might imply.

Additionally, my mother told me in my adulthood that my father had confided to her that he had trouble dating black women because they reminded him of his sisters, and it felt incestuous. Interestingly, Noni married a man with the same nickname as my father, Bunny. I have been curious about the nature of my father's relationship with Noni. Although I never sensed that there was any overt sexual interaction, I wonder if a more subtle, less conscious attachment and/or fantasy lived between them that also led my father to my mother. He was able to have a romantic, passionate relationship with a "Noni look-alike" from a safe distance, a race away, without risking incestuous feelings.

As an adult, my father's passionate energy led him to become active in Leftist politics. In due course, he volunteered for the Abraham Lincoln Brigade, a multi-racial cadre of United States' soldiers who chose to fight in Spain against Fascism in the Spanish Civil War of the 1930s. The Lincoln Brigade was the American contingent of soldiers within the global International Brigades fighting to halt Fascist troops in Spain and thereby avert their infiltration of all of Europe. These soldiers fought in Spain in violation of the neutrality policy of the US government toward the escalating conflict in Europe, and were disciplined by the federal courts upon their return. The conflict between the Spanish Republicans already elected to govern Spain and Franco's Nationalist armies who were attempting a coup presaged the eventuality of World War II. Had the Brigades succeeded in Spain, the Second World War might have been prevented.

In Spain, my father befriended Langston Hughes, the renowned writer, playwright, and poet, who was there as a journalist, and they developed a lifelong connection. During the lengthy siege of Madrid by Franco's armies from 1936-1939, my father drove a truck at night, carrying supplies across the Pyrenees from France to Spain to support the Republic and providing transport for Langston Hughes across enemy lines. At one point during wartime, while my father and Langston were walking in France in winter, Langston, who did not have a warm coat, complained of the bitter cold. My father, without a moment's thought, took off his own long coat and gave it to him. Here was the kind, compassionate side of my father to which my mother was attracted and through which I felt loved and safe. Always there, it nonetheless became obscured by his hurt and anger as time progressed.

As an aside, when I was in my thirties and vacationing at a resort with a friend, the television was on in our hotel room. For some reason, I abruptly looked up to see an old photo on the screen of my father and Langston Hughes standing together and talking. The TV show was a documentary on Langston Hughes, and the photo was one I remembered seeing at home. Seeing it suddenly in that context was surreal!

After Madrid fell to Fascism in 1939 and the International Brigades were withdrawn, my father joined a group of soldiers in climbing the Pyrenees to France in order to return to the States. Along the way he suffered a serious laceration on his leg that became infected. He was spared a death from gangrene by a female physician in Paris who risked her life and freedom to treat him and other injured Brigadiers in an underground treatment center. He always felt deeply indebted to this brave young woman. Once back home, my father volunteered for World War II. He was too old to be drafted, but he wanted to continue fighting against Fascism, as his younger brothers were. He passed the exam to attend Officer's Candidate School with a high score but was not allowed to do so because of his involvement in Spain and his race. Black soldiers, then, could not hold authority over white soldiers in the military or have the special training that OCS extended. He also had his passport revoked at one point as a sanction for his involvement in Spain.

Undeterred in his wish to fight for democracy, my father joined the Army as a private, rose quickly to rank of sergeant, but lost that rank after going AWOL to marry my mother in 1943. The Army had given him leave, during which he and my mother had planned to marry, but the Army rescinded it at the last moment…while my father was waiting for the train. He ignored the demand to return to his post, and my parents were married. When he did return at the end of his leave, he was demoted. My father was not upset about the loss of rank, however, because he felt more aligned with the privates than with their superiors; he did not like wielding power over others, especially those with whom he identified. He also was happy that his bond with my mother was now a marriage. Nonetheless as it evolved, my father's choice to fight for his country when he did not have to do so, particularly as a private, marked the remainder of his life.

My father entered World War II with a zeal to fight for "good," to stand up for the democratic values of his country as his brothers were doing, and to follow through on the anti-Fascist commitment that he had made in Spain. He left the military with a battered body and soul, badly injured, deeply disillusioned about the value of war, and angry at the racial prejudice that was endemic in the military. He lost his closest "battle buddy," Gus, in a foxhole when a bomb exploded near Gus, splattering my father with blood, gore, and Gus's body fragments. I remember my father having nightmares about Gus, screaming for his mother, and crying in his sleep, and my mother trying to comfort him.

Tragically, my father was gravely wounded in Italy in 1945, sustaining a shattered left leg and almost losing his life. He refused amputation but suffered through six surgeries that left him able to walk, but crippled and in almost constant pain. He also was thought to be sterile from the frequent x-rays he received, and his mental health was compromised for the rest of his life from what was later known to be PTSD. When he returned from war, disabled and traumatized after fighting for the United States, blacks were segregated in the South and discriminated against in the North. Jim Crow laws that denied blacks (Negroes or coloreds at that time) civil rights and personal dignity dominated the South, whereas more covert prejudice influenced attitudes in the North. During the McCarthy Era, my father was blacklisted from working in New York State because of his involvement in the Spanish Civil War. Bunny was enraged at the racial and social inequities for himself and others, and he constantly hurt physically and emotionally. He walked with metal braces connected to his arms and could only slightly bend his left knee. He could not work at any physical job. He fumed with frustration.

My father experienced his years in the Army as laden with personal conflict, not just the repercussions of combat. As he wrote to my mother at one point during his service, interpersonal experiences with other soldiers and his command were fraught with pleasure followed by insult, embraces followed by kicks in the ass, and kisses followed by being spit upon. Eventually, although not right away, after years of fighting in war and in peace for humanistic principles, my father's hold on hope and determination faltered. His visions for social humanism and equality became infected by his emergent clarity about the intransigence of American racism and injustice. It might be understood that, on a very unconscious level, his injured left leg was entwined with his blemished Leftist ideals. From being a man who walked through life with a steady footing, he lived after the war physically and psychologically off-balance.

The sequelae of my father's disability and my presence as an only child colored much of our family life. My parents lived modestly and within the constraints imposed by my father's physical and later emotional considerations. Yet, as an only child who came late in my parents' lives, I was adored and indulged by the three adults around me. My mother was essential to the family stability, but she did not dominate. Nor did her mother, who entered our household after I was born to care for me. My parents' marriage was sometimes strained but always held firm. I never had concerns that they would separate, and I never perceived a lack of love between them. Decades before the concept of PTSD was introduced, my mother had a deep appreciation of the effect of early trauma and later war experiences on my father's mental health. She understood my father and his vulnerabilities far better than she understood me and mine. My mother wasn't oblivious or in denial about everything, but with me she had a blind spot about race. She was loving but color-blind, unable to see the complexion of things.

My middle-class home was secure, but the history of my family and our socio-cultural environment was often unforgiving. While my father stayed home and tried to recover from his war injury and his emotional distress, my mother worked full-time as a medical assistant/lab technician/secretary for a physician in private practice in Manhattan, a job she held for thirty-five years. During this time, my father shifted from being a social drinker to managing his physical and emotional pain with spurts of heavy drinking. Time spent in local taverns, sometimes among other war veterans, partly assuaged his anger and masked the humiliation that he felt in being a disabled black man unable to provide for his family. When my mother was pregnant with me, my father decided that he had to walk without braces because he would not be able to hold his baby using braces. So, with grit and determination, he shifted to crutches and later to a cane, which made him more mobile. But he was never able to walk freely or comfortably.

Later, my father would take me with him sometimes to the local tavern, making me sit at a table with a Shirley Temple instead of spinning on the barstools as I desired, because "Ladies do not sit at the bar." So I sat quietly with my ginger ale and Maraschino cherry, watching my father interact with his "buddies" over a few beers. From today's perspective, this might be judged as an inappropriate activity for a young child, but it gave me an appreciation for the value of being near a parent without direct interaction, just absorbing the demeanor of the parent and the culture of adulthood from afar. I still have nostalgia for older bars with wooden counters, bar stools that spin, and the ever-present smell of liquor.

In contrast to Bunny, my mother, Helen, was a woman of average height with straight brown hair and a pretty and pleasing but unassuming countenance that matched her personality. The younger of two girls from a Midwestern German-Irish, upper-middle class, educated Catholic family, she came to New York City following her sister, Rosemary, who was studying concert piano at The Juilliard School. My maternal grandfather, Max Muenich, was a lawyer from a family of farmers, physicians, and attorneys originally from Wisconsin. He refused to litigate divorces because of his Catholic beliefs, a choice that compromised his financial status, as divorces were a major source of income for lawyers at the time.

In 1912, Max married my grandmother, Clara Rose, the second of three daughters—the only son and youngest child in the family having died from "diarrhea" as a toddler. Max and Clara soon had two girls in close succession and no other children, a somewhat odd circumstance for a Catholic family in that era, but the reason for this is not known to me. My mother's parents weathered the Great Depression relatively unscathed, although my grandmother did take a job to supplement my grandfather's income. For a few years my grandmother worked for Coca-Cola, planning and supervising field trips for school children to the bottling company. In the 1920s Midwestern setting in which Rosemary and Helen grew up, Rosemary was likely a local child music prodigy. She was invited to study piano in Italy at eighteen and did spend time there before attending Juilliard.

In coming to New York City, my mother hoped to dance with a ballet company. From her Missouri origin in 1916 within a traditional family, my mother quickly became an ardent New Yorker. For her entire lifetime, she loved the energy, culture, and intellectual liveliness of New York City. My mother almost completed a college degree in Physics from Hunter College, except for a required Physical Education course that she refused to take at night after a full day's work. She became engaged to a wealthy Italian man who owned a small Greek island but broke the engagement after meeting my father. Decades later, she attended this man's funeral. For a while, my mother danced with Ballet Russe de Monte Carlo, the forerunner of American Ballet Theatre, but the conflicts in Europe in the mid-1930s shortened the ballet season to only a few weeks. Eventually, her dancing career was aborted by WWII, which interrupted cultural performances of all kinds all over the world. By the time the war ended and the ballet companies were revitalized, my mother was too old to dance professionally. A great disappointment in her life.

My parents met through a political organization in New York City, fell in love, married in 1943, and I, their only child, was born in 1954 after my parents had resigned themselves to being childless. They were married by Adam Clayton Powell Sr., knew Paul Robeson, and were social activists for much of their adult lives from union organizing to Civil Rights to anti-War movements. My maternal grandparents, who were Democrats but rather apolitical, eventually came to New York City to be near their daughters. They resided in Manhattan and made some peripheral connections to the social justice politics movements that so excited my parents.

My grandparents liked my father and welcomed him, although my grandfather warned my mother that she was "choosing a very hard life" in marrying a Negro (the proper term of the day). My grandfather died soon thereafter before I could know him, thus creating space for my grandmother, Clara, to later live with us and care for me. By the time I was born, my mother was employed full-time, and my father was attending college. In placing me largely in my grandmother's care, my mother unconsciously gave me her mother, an act of love entangled with other more complex needs and motives. Clara became my beloved "Nanny," and eventually the namesake of my daughter. Nanny was gracious, reserved, endlessly patient with me, and a primary source of emotional calm and security in our sometimes-strained household. She has remained the only person in my life toward whom I have felt only love, never any ambivalence.

When I was born, my parents lived in the Marble Hill projects in the Bronx for about one year. I have no clear memory of our apartment in the Bronx, but I remember our next home well. In the next years of my life, the four of us—my parents, me, and Nanny, along with the family dog, Tassie—moved to a large apartment in Washington Heights that overlooked the Hudson River and George Washington Bridge with a wide panoramic view. We lived there until I was six. Large French doors that connected the hall to the living and dining rooms, bare wood floors on which I rode my tricycle watched by Nanny, a kitchen with red plaid curtains, my bedroom with decals on pink walls and a gray-speckled crib with a lamb painted on the headboard. The feeling of these images is warmth and safety.

I particularly recall my father walking with me through the dark, scary basement of our building, up some stairs, emerging in a store on the adjacent street that sold sundries. He would buy a newspaper and cigarettes, the New York Times and Herbert Tareytons, of course, and the store owner would give me candy or ice cream from large cardboard freezer barrels of Breyer's. It was a great adventure! I further recall being mesmerized by the lights on the George Washington Bridge and in the towns of the Palisades across the river. My father would pick me up and hold me to the window to point out the lights. I also remember being dazzled watching the street lights at night from the rear window or while sitting in the jumper seat of the large black-and-yellow checkered cabs that were ubiquitous in Manhattan.

During these early years, I attended a local nursery school after my parents felt that I did not have enough interaction with other children. I remember enjoying nursery school, learning to write numbers and letters, playing, and swimming in a small wading pool in the summertime. To get there from our apartment, it was necessary to walk up a "big hill." It was an effort for me to climb this hill, but when I saw it as an adult it is really a small incline. In the winter, though, the wind would blow from the Hudson River and push me, and I would call out to my grandmother who shepherded me back and forth to school: *"Save me, Nanny, save me!"* She would wrap me under her arm with her big fur coat with a silk lining, and we would continue on. She also brought me a Tootsie Roll every afternoon when she picked me up, and I would marvel that sometimes (in the cold weather) it was hard, and sometimes (in the warm weather) it was soft and mushy.

As a pre-schooler, I also took modern dance classes with a teacher whom my mother knew, named "Blanche," a name perhaps worthy of note. During some summers I spent time with my mother and grandmother in a rented cottage in Vermont while my father remained in Manhattan with Tassie. When we returned from one Vermont trip, my father had made a large "Welcome Home" banner and hung it in the foyer of the apartment. He had missed us! He and Tassie were delighted to see us, and I was delighted to see both of them. I remember my excitement and my father's big smile.

Tassie, my friend and confidante for most of my childhood, started out as Nanny's dog whom she had cared for since she was a tiny puppy. She was a gift to Nanny from my aunt Rosemary. As the story goes, as a young puppy Tassie developed pneumonia, and my grandmother kept her alive by holding her close to her chest all day and sleeping with her in an armchair until she recovered. Tassie lived to be sixteen, loved by all of us. Through that time I experienced her as more human than not. When I was a young child, she was definitely more Self than Other. As an interesting aside, Tassie was half Beagle and half Welsh Terrier, a mixed-breed dog…another "coincidence" perhaps worthy of note.

Among my early Manhattan memories are different and more disturbing recollections that reflect the complexities of my family, the racial tenor of the times, and the complicated emotional threads that came to define me. One day as Nanny and I were leaving our apartment building, a woman tried to close the large outer door on me, forcing my grandmother to snatch me away just in time. I have a mental picture of the green-tiled lobby floor and the black ironwork on the tall, heavy glass door as it closed in on me. I felt fear and confusion as my beloved grandmother yanked me painfully by my arm to escape the door. *Why was Nanny hurting me???* Later in my life, I learned that the woman who had closed the door harbored racial hatred that she had expressed to my parents before. This time she directed her rage physically toward a young child.

Another recollection stamped into my memory: the intensity of my father's anger around racial discrimination and his PTSD-related reactivity. At age four, I fell off of the top bunk of a young friend's bunk bed and split my tongue with my teeth. My friend's mother rushed me to the nearby hospital, where my parents met me. After examining me, the white doctor told my father that he would not stitch my tongue, which my father heard as being unwilling to do so because I was not white. My father grabbed the doctor by his lab coat and pushed him against a wall, telling him forcefully that he WOULD stitch my tongue. Luckily, the doctor had a clear mind and spoke quietly to my father explaining that my tongue would heal without stitches, and my father calmed down. I remember feeling the tension in the room, the pain of my tongue, a sense of danger, and my own confusion. This was my first awareness that my father was different in a distressing way and my first glimpse of the PTSD that would soon encroach on our family life.

Struggling painfully with his disability, my father always had a marked limp and could not fully bend one knee. His crutches or cane partly compensated for his poor balance, and a very elevated heavy shoe partly disguised the large discrepancy between the length of his legs. Nonetheless, he was obviously disabled, but the worst ravages of PTSD from both the war and his earlier life had yet to surface. I did not notice his disability and just adored him for his boundless warmth and love for me. I did not see his suffering—I just happily snuggled into the security and affection that he offered. I remember the doctor incident as the first tiny crack in that cocoon.

My father's favorite spot in our house, and the favorite spot of Tassie, was a living room armchair by a window, next to a "hi-fi," the sound system of the day. There he would drink Rheingold beer and smoke Herbert Tareyton cigarettes, read, listen to albums of musicians such as Louis Armstrong, Harry Belafonte, and Maurice Chevalier and sometimes sing along if he had a beer or two. Tassie would lie right next to him and sometimes nudge him out of the chair so that she could have it to herself. The music evoked my father's nostalgia and melancholia, and sometimes, after a few more beers, he would weep. As a very young child, I cried when he played Harry Belafonte's song "Kingston Town." I heard the lyrics of "I had to leave a little girl in Kingston

Town" as "I had to leave [my] little girl in Kingston Town" and sometimes felt sadness and loss along with him.

Children were a source of delight for my father, especially the joy and abandon he saw in them. He was not strict and by no means a disciplinarian, nor was he particularly good at supervising children because he was quite comfortable giving them a free rein to do whatever. He would just watch and smile and sometimes chuckle to himself, enjoying their unabashed liveliness. Later in his life, he could be irritated by noise and commotion, but the pleasure that my father saw children take in the world around them seemed to be an antidote to his own despondency.

My father's entire life was laced with trauma. Family circumstances, childhood poverty, the experience of being black in the early decades of the 20th century and the long Jim Crow era, his lifelong efforts to fight social injustice, his war experiences, and the devastating impact of his war injury on the quality of his life carved furrows of rage, grief, and harsh disappointment on the otherwise, loving, warm personality of a brilliant, well-educated, and remarkably well-read man who generously extended affection and support. Alongside a caring and principled social consciousness, my father's anger, chronic physical pain, and combat trauma eventually coalesced into PTSD. As is true for many PTSD sufferers, he increasingly found an outlet in alcohol.

Over the years, especially in the years after the war, during which he was home alone while my mother worked, a sporadic indulgence in beer and whiskey became less sporadic until my father settled into a pattern of weekend binge drinking to relieve his pain. By the time I was in elementary school and he was fully employed, alcohol brought strident, harsh emotions into the foreground and created tension in our household. My parents did not fight frequently, but my father's drinking released his anger and despair, stressing us all.

By this time in his life, Bunny worked responsibly at a professional job all week and did not drink excessively on weekdays. However, he would drink heavily through the weekends. On weekdays when my father came home from work, he would settle into "his chair," have a beer and a cigarette, read the New York Times and the local newspapers, and then read whatever non-fiction book had his attention. When my mother returned from work an hour or so later, they would have dinner together. I would usually have dinner earlier with my grandmother. After dinner, we would generally watch TV as a family, or my parents would talk. Nanny, Tassie, and I would go to bed, and they would stay downstairs, read, and watch the eleven o'clock news.

But on Friday evenings, my father would have more beers and whiskey, turn on the hi-fi at high volume, and start a weekend binge. Intense political conversations frequently resounded in our living room between my parents or sometimes with their friends. Many of these discussions were intelligent and thoughtful when my father was sober, but when he was drinking, they tended to be more irascible than just friendly conversation, more tirade than discourse. When sober, my father was dignified and highly respectable, but when drinking he was sarcastic, sometimes crass, loud, irritable, and difficult.

Never was my father physically aggressive, but routinely he combined Rheingold beer, Johnnie Walker Red Label whiskey, cigarettes, and loud music with the cumulative griefs, pains, losses, and disappointments of his life. This concoction allowed him to express his frustration and rage in rants about racial prejudice, politics, the abuses and horrors of war, the lies perpetrated about American history and actions of the US government. As I grew older, though, I realized that listening to him, however unpleasant at times, had been an education in itself. To distract me when he was drinking, my grandmother often would bring me into her room and involve me in activities, such as "sewing a quilt," or playing with a felt board that she made for me, or reading a book. That was one of her many expressions of love and protection. My father would mingle his love with his obnoxious drunkenness by coming into my bedroom in the middle of the night intoxicated, turning on the light, jostling my bed, disturbing my sleep by singing old songs to me, such as Maurice Chevalier's "Thank Heaven for Little Girls" and "Gigi." Louis Armstrong's "Hello Dolly" and Nat King Cole's "Walking My Baby Back Home" were also standards in his midnight repertoire. My mother would offer the suggestion, in her words, that I "turn off [my] ears." Making myself deaf was something I never learned to do.

Apart from their interracial marriage, my father's alcohol problem, and the fact that my mother was the primary breadwinner for quite a few years, my parents lived an otherwise conventional life. They worked, raised me with love and support, paid bills responsibly, owned a modest home, saved money, had friends, and maintained a long and loving marriage. However, they also had a socialistic and atheistic bent, and radical (in the context of the times) political views. I remember hearing my mother remark to my father on the day that Kennedy was killed: "This was done by the CIA…no one else could organize this." Now that is an ordinary thought, but then, when the USA was revered, it was akin to blasphemy. My father also would give a lecture at Thanksgiving dinners about the falsity of the Thanksgiving story. To him, the Thanksgiving celebration served to belie the reality that the settlers slaughtered American Indians (in the vernacular at the time)…and even if one shared meal did occur, it did not compensate for the decimation of the American Indian population and cultures. Again, an evolving awareness now that sixty-five years ago was suggested by almost no one.

My mother's gentler, calmer nature was shaped by a near-fatal tragedy that occurred soon after her birth. When she was born in 1916, visitors came to see her, the new baby. During one such a visit, her two-year-old sister, Rosemary, fell down the cellar stairs and hit her head. A few days later, Rosemary complained to my grandmother that her head hurt. My grandmother took her to the local family doctor who bore the grim news that Rosemary had a "blood clot on her brain," a cerebral hematoma that had to be removed or she would die. Well, this was 1916…no special hospitals, no neurosurgery for toddlers, no specialized surgeons.

The family doctor removed the hematoma himself in the local hospital and sent Rosemary home with the admonition to her parents that she could not run, jump, or play actively for at least one year. Her skull was still growing, so he could not cover it with a metal plate, and if she hit her head again she would likely die. So my grandmother was charged with the care of a toddler who had to be kept still for a year and a newborn baby. The doctor came to the house daily to check the bandages around Rosemary's skull, and in my grandmother's telling Rosemary would scream and cry as soon as she heard his horse-and-buggy turn down their road. My grandmother must have been worried and overwhelmed all of the time.

My aunt developed a remarkable intellect and was highly accomplished in an era when very smart women did not have a place. She earned her degree from Juilliard in classical piano, and then received a Ph.D. in Economics, a Ph.D. in Art History, and completed everything but a dissertation for a Ph.D. in Chemistry, all from Columbia University. She also developed some fluency in a few languages relevant to the study of Art History. At some point, Rosemary stopped playing the piano totally because she "couldn't be the best," but she kept a grand piano all of her life. I imagine Rosemary as a toddler lying in her bed, frustrated, restless, and confined, turning to her thoughts and intellect to occupy herself. As psychoanalysts might say, she cathected her brain and her mind. The injured brain of her childhood became an ever-active mind throughout her adulthood.

Rosemary was outspoken, strong-willed, and something of a perfectionist. She also was intolerant of any dependency. She married three times, twice to Jewish men and married her third husband with the understanding that she would not be involved in the care of his two school-aged children. And she was not, despite their presence in the home. I believe that my aunt's accident shaped my mother's character very early. My mother, Helen, intuited from the cradle that the way to have her needs met under the circumstance was not to ask for too much from her mother. If she was easily satisfied and did not assert her needs unnecessarily, she would be well-attended. But the care and attention that Rosemary required meant that there was not a lot of extra. Helen could not have known or understood this cognitively in her early months of life, but infants can and do absorb the sense of things, coming to "know" the nature of their emotional environment. Being mild-mannered, keeping a low profile, and not protesting unnecessarily was the way for my mother to go, a path that she followed all of her life.

While Rosemary, by temperament and circumstance, drove the household with her forceful personality, Helen settled for the back seat. My mother was intelligent, strong, loyal, and highly competent, but self-effacing, slow to anger, and sometimes annoyingly selfless. Sometimes I thought that she had no personal needs. Her relationship with her sister was intermittently close and frayed until the last decades of Rosemary's life when they shared time and sisterly intimacy. My aunt died suddenly in her eighties of a ruptured stomach artery while having coffee with my mother one morning, seated near the grand piano in her New York City apartment.

My grandmother, who died from congestive heart failure at eighty-seven as I began graduate school, maintained relationships with both of her daughters. To her credit, she adapted remarkably well to their life choices, choices that jarringly opposed her devout Catholic background. She negotiated the tension between Self and Other in this part of her life with grace and dignity, never imposing her perspectives but never relinquishing them. To her, the most important factor was that everyone has a soul, and she must have kept that in the forefront of her mind as she wrestled with the unexpected. Nanny never could have thought as a young Midwestern Catholic woman in the early 1900s that she would end up in New York City from Missouri, that one of her children would marry three times, twice to Jewish men, and have multiple abortions, and that the other would become an atheist, marry a black Socialist who drank too much, and give her a mixed-race grandchild. She must have had her private moments of distress, disappointment, and worry, but she rose to the challenge and loved all of us well.

My mother adored "the City" all of her adult life. She was in New York City, and New York City was in her. In the 1950s and early 1960s, before it was overtaken by the wealthy, New York City, and Manhattan in particular, consisted largely of middle-class communities dotted with poor and rich enclaves. People leased their apartments for ten, fifteen, twenty years establishing solid family neighborhoods. Under rent control, Manhattan was ethnically diverse and culturally rich, if not socially integrated. Throughout my childhood, my mother exposed me to its cultural riches. From seeing the "Nutcracker" at Lincoln Center and 5th Avenue department stores with their remarkable holiday displays every Christmas, to children's theater, dance and music performances, the zoos, Central Park, Orchard Beach, horseback riding at Van Cortlandt Park and ice skating at Rockefeller Center, the Statue of Liberty, museums, FAO Schwartz, nice restaurants as well as Horn and Hardart Automat and Schraffts, and the subway, my mother showed me its magic. My father kept me aware of the poverty, despair, and injustice that also were New York City.

Credit should be given to my Aunt Rosemary, who doggedly urged my father to go to college after the war years. In anger and hopelessness, he resisted, but she pushed him to understand that he had a very good mind that was going to waste, and that doing intellectual work was the best path forward. Although his body was badly compromised, his intellect was superior. Eventually following my aunt's advice, my father attended Columbia University on the GI bill, receiving a BA in Anthropology and a MA in Library Science. He attended library school after being given the choice by the VA to be trained as a tailor or to be educated as a librarian. The nature of his disability did not allow him to seek training for any other employment at government expense. So, wisely, my father selected the latter option.

There is a poignant parallel between an early experience of my father at Columbia and his later profession. As a freshman student, my father was forty years old, visibly handicapped, and black, among mostly young and healthy white college students. He was self-conscious and unsure of himself as a college student. His first English assignment required him go to the university library and research some material for a paper. When my father approached the library, facing him was a large brick building with wide stairs set between tall white pillars. He did not see how he could climb the stairs with his arm braces. In addition to presenting physical obstacles, the white-pillared stairs at this white-and-brick imposing building also represented the white intellectual community and the white historical tradition of Columbia from which my father's ancestors had been excluded. My father felt intimidated and could not enter the library. Being resourceful and not a quitter, he returned home and wrote his paper about his inability to enter the library instead of the assigned topic, and the paper was accepted by the professor. My father's Library Science degree a few years later was an actual and a symbolic achievement.

After graduating from Columbia, my father took a job as a librarian in Bridgeport, Connecticut. Being blacklisted during the McCarthy Era for his participation in the Spanish Civil War rendered him ineligible to work in New York State in such a position. The career of a librarian, however, was not a bad professional fit. The library met his intellectual needs and allowed him a good deal of interaction with others. He was able to incorporate his passion for books into his work, he could sit at a desk and work rather than having to stand or walk, and his speciality as a Catalog and Reference Librarian was interesting and expanded his knowledge. Before computers, my father was the guy one approached to find out specific information or where to find information among the extensive library resources. He also was responsible for selecting books for the library, which fit well with his love for reading. The downside of this first job was that he had to take a one-and-a-half hour train ride between Bridgeport and Manhattan. And he had to manage the train station and the train on crutches or with a cane. This was exhausting and exacerbated his mental stress and his physical pain.

Through Columbia, life experiences, and his own self-education, my father knew something about almost everything. He read voraciously. He held strong opinions about which he could argue cogently and vehemently. He knew and appreciated different cultural perspectives, all the while sustaining an awareness of the pain endemic to the human condition. He spoke Spanish competently and read French fluently. I have a few vivid memories of him reading political books in French that were not available in English. Bunny was a literate man with deep-seated values and principles and an astute thinker. These qualities made him unusual, but they also made him vulnerable to frustration and rage. Yet he retained a good sense of humor, an open-hearted generosity, and an enjoyment and appreciation of people that, despite his drinking and anger, shone through his trauma and pain.

The following anecdote captures my father's generosity, his sensitivity to the distress of others, and the manner in which my mother's measured judgement balanced some of his admirable, but reckless, inspirations. Once when I was about nine, my father brought home a strange black man whom he had encountered on the street. The man told my father that he did not have food, so my father invited him for dinner. He ate dinner with us, which I found quite strange, and then, as he did not have a place to sleep, my father offered him to stay overnight, which I found even more peculiar. My mother was not pleased with that idea but said nothing in the moment. After we were all in bed, she told my father that she was happy to have made dinner for this stranger, but that it was not safe for him to be in the house while we were all sleeping. That we did not know him at all, that I was in the house, and that his presence posed a potential danger to everyone. She requested that my father ask him to leave. So, in the middle of the night, my father woke the man up, and he left quietly. Nonetheless, as he opened the front door, my father handed him two twenty dollar bills, a good amount of money in those days.

When I was about to enter elementary school, my parents decided to explore other options that might be easier than my father's work commute and open up school options for me. My parents had hoped that I could attend Hunter College Elementary School, a public elementary school in Manhattan for gifted students. However, although I passed the academic assessment portion of the admissions process, I was very shy and did not speak to people readily, making the interview portion difficult. Private school was too expensive and too far from my parents' personal beliefs and ideologies, and public school was not academically up to their standards. So my parents had to look elsewhere for acceptable educational opportunities. They turned to suburban New Jersey.

At that time, the suburbs of Newark presented some possibilities. The location had to be within commuting distance of my mother's job near Grand Central Station in Manhattan, it had to be racially integrated with appropriate housing, and it had to offer a good public school system. My father took a job in one such suburb as a librarian in a public library, but he had great difficulty finding suitable housing. Decent homes were "whites only" and the homes available to "Negroes or coloreds" were substandard. For a year, he commuted from New Jersey to Manhattan every weekend but spent weekdays in New

Jersey working and looking for a place for us all to live. After this year, when I was six, he found a housing situation in the ground floor of a comfortable house owned by a middle-class black couple who lived upstairs. I remember this house, the upstairs owners, and the neighborhood, but I also remember the sleepwalking episodes I had when we first moved there. These episodes were experiences of being Other to my Self, dislocated, disconnected, and, for a brief period, dissociated.

The first time that I walked in my sleep I actually went outside of the house. I remember waking up a few houses down from our house, looking down at my white pajamas with red trim. It was probably about dawn, not dark, but not sunny yet. I walked back home and knocked on the door for what seemed like a long time before my father came to the door. He was taken aback and puzzled as to why I hadn't rung the doorbell. I was confused. Coming from a New York City apartment with a knocker: *What's a doorbell???* The second time I indulged in a midnight stroll I stayed inside but started down the basement steps. I awoke to find my mother next to me gently leading me back upstairs. She must have heard me get up and followed me. I do not remember my thoughts, except that it felt strange not to know what happened. It must have been disorienting to be in a suburban neighborhood and a house after only knowing city streets and apartment buildings.

After about one year, my parents bought their first home near the same area. It was a simple duplex less than a block from the bus stop, convenient for my mother, and within walking distance or a short bus ride to the library where my father was employed. At the time, the local school system was highly rated. There was even a Catholic church nearby for my grandmother to attend. The neighborhood housed middle-class families, many with young children, and the elementary and junior high schools were just a few blocks away. It was racially integrated with black, Italian, and Jewish families living in unpretentious but generally well cared-for homes. An elderly Italian widower and an old Italian shoemaker lived on opposing corners of our street. Both spoke broken English but were friendly and spent time talking with the neighborhood children.

We lived on one side of a brand-new duplex with the first black principal of an all-white suburban school with his family in the other side of the duplex, and a physical therapist and his family in the house next door on the other side. Many summer evenings were spent playing with other children while our parents watered their lawns. Many of the parents, mine included, put great effort into the gardens and lawns, and the results up and down the street were pleasing to the eye. My mother had wanted to buy a house in the other side of town with larger, older homes, front porches, and mature landscaping, but my father wanted something new. He had spent all of his life with hand-me-downs, old things, settling for whatever was available, and he wanted a fresh start. My mother, not surprisingly, acquiesced. So the small house in which I grew up and my mother lived until her eighties was the final choice. It was comfortable and attractive enough with good-sized front and back yards, but it lacked charm or any special features.

My school was a short walking distance away from home, and I walked to school each day. My parents left for work in the morning and were home in the evening. Sometimes I met one or both of them at the corner bus stop. During the school day, I walked home and Nanny gave me lunch. After school, I played with neighborhood children at one of our homes or at games in the street. We played "until the streetlights came on" and, if necessary, went to the nearest home to use the bathroom or get a drink of water. We got glimpses of the interiors of many homes and of the lifestyles that were lived by our peers. Most of the parents were friendly and welcoming. There was little homework until late in elementary school, no consistent adult supervision, and little suspicion of adults. I, like my father, was a voracious reader and would bring books outside and read on my front steps. My classes, like my neighborhood, were racially integrated, and the education was good. But racial tensions were palpable. Dark clouds were gathering.

II

THE EMERGENCE OF DESPAIR

My experiences living in suburban New Jersey were much more painful than my early years in Manhattan, mostly because of class and racial issues that began to dominate my life. Because both of my parents worked and my father was a professional, they had more economic assets than many of the families around me, even though our lifestyles were overtly similar. Their relative financial ease allowed me more and different experiences than those of my peers. My complexion and hair texture were ambiguous but most often were perceived as white. I was an excellent student, an avid reader, and teachers almost always liked me. However, except for riding horses as a teenager and young adult, I was a mediocre athlete at best. My parents were older, interracially married, my mother was employed outside of her home, my father was visibly handicapped, and I had no siblings—very unusual family demographics for the early 1960s. As my parents were non-believers, there was no religious affiliation to offer a community or source of identity. I was clearly different, and in the eyes of my peers, not in a good way. At best, I was an object of curiosity, and in my local community usually an object of derision. As I understood later, I was also an object of envy. However, an underlying dynamic with my mother left room for these experiences of difference to burrow into my psyche.

It took many years of psychoanalysis for me to grasp the qualities in my relationship with my mother that left me vulnerable, but in my thirties it became clear. Or at least I developed a narrative that fits our history and my feelings. Until then, especially as a child, I just felt frightened, lonely, and confused—caught within race and class conflicts that were embedded in our society but beyond my comprehension. My mother was an object of both my desire and rage. It seemed to me that she held a solution to my dilemma and pain, but she kept it to herself; she and the depth of her affection were close but just beyond my grasp. Color didn't matter to my mother, so why was it so painful to me? What was her secret? She loved me, so why didn't she help me? As a child, the answers to these questions came down to my inadequacy, my defectiveness. That is a child's egocentric perspective. Understanding my mother as a separate person with her own flaws and failings came decades later. Much of what I will describe here about my mother was most likely unconscious on her part, but she did at one point after the birth of my daughter acknowledge glimmers of understanding. I must detour for a moment to elaborate the backstory that is a frame for all that is to come.

My mother was attracted to my father by his warmth and passion, his open and loving nature, his intelligence, and his moral steadfastness. To this, she would agree. Yet, I believe that his color allowed her an avenue of rebellion from her reserved, white, Midwestern, Catholic upbringing—a rebellion that she had never before allowed herself. It also gave her an opportunity to "one-up" her sister by becoming even more outrageous than Rosemary. An unconscious satisfaction. My father encouraged my mother to engage in left-leaning politics, to be more spontaneous than was her inclination, and he exposed her to novel ideas and perspectives. She modeled responsibility, dependability, and restraint for him. They fell in love, and in many ways it was a good match.

Helen and Bunny sustained a lasting bond around intellectual interests, humanitarian values, common political views, and mutual respect, and my mother came to understand my father deeply, As he once admitted to me, she "kept me [my father] on the right track," demanding family responsibility and commitment from him, which he gave. Yet, in leaving her wealthy Italian fiance after meeting my father, my mother landed in a passionate relationship with someone with few financial resources, whose career trajectory was very unclear, and who was exciting to her but not the most stable choice. As she once told me: "We thought we could live on love." There was much more difficulty ahead than either of my parents first realized.

From hostility from my father's family more than my mother's, and the withdrawal of friends, to a few dangerous encounters with hostile strangers, their lives as an interracial couple were not easy. This situation was, of course, compounded by my father's disability and heavy drinking, and the emotional strain that those generated. Through my own psychoanalysis in my young adulthood, I came to an understanding that my mother may have been less sanguine about having a child with a black man than she was about marrying one. Unconsciously, bearing a mixed-race child was perhaps a bridge too far. She rose to the occasion and was a good mother, but her deepest feelings about motherhood and about me were mixed. I doubt that she had a strong personal desire to be a mother. She would have been fine just with my father. This was not true for my father, who wanted a large family. I believe that her unconscious ambivalence was built into my psyche from before my birth, that it is an essential part of me. It originated as Other to me, but became Other-in-Self. It manifested in qualities of our early attachment bond, which is the essential ingredient of my generally melancholic mood state.

I expressed this at the age of two when, reportedly, I sat on the kitchen floor near both of my parents and said: "I'm sad." My father asked: "Why are you sad, honey?" I answered: "I don't know. I just sad." Although I can feel happy and optimistic, I cannot sustain these feelings. They evaporate. For me, a glass is half-empty, and on a beautiful sunny day my focus is drawn to the clouds on the horizon rather than to the sunlight. There may a light at the end of the tunnel, but there is always a tunnel at the end of the light. A year or so later, I found a partial solution to my sadness. I created an imaginary companion named Ethel, after a white friend of my mother. In my mind's eye, Ethel was white, partly Self and partly Other. She reflected my identification with my white mother divorced from any black identifications that I had developed. Yet, I gave her an unattractive name that possibly reflected a subliminal sense of feeling ugly and unlovable.

My parents had hoped unsuccessfully for eleven years to conceive, decades before there were many fertility treatments or options. When my father was told that his sperm were damaged, poorly formed from the many X-rays he had received on his leg, there was no longer any expectation of a pregnancy. However, my mother had an abortion in her early twenties, the details of which I do not know, and she did feel that she was able to conceive. And at age thirty-seven, considered quite old for first motherhood during that era, she did. For my father, this likely was a wonderful surprise that affirmed his viability as a man in the context of his emasculating disability.

My mother, though, did not realize that she was pregnant until about her fourth month, probably when she felt movement. In her telling of this story, she emphasized her and my father's delight at the news. My father honestly acknowledged being nervous the whole time that "the baby would have two heads" or that the baby would be a boy with whom he could not run, play ball, or wrestle. He was concerned that his damaged sperm would create an anomaly or that he could not be the father that he wished to be because of his other physical defects. He might have been concerned that this wonderful event would be tarnished for him by underscoring his defects or simply taken from him, rather than accentuating his masculine well-being. Perhaps the inner sense of being "defective," which I carried deep in my psyche until my analysis, parallels his experience of himself and is not just an artifact of my unconscious connection with my mother.

Both my father's excitement and his worry jibes with my experience of him, though I suspect that my mother's feelings were more ambivalent than pure delight. Another example of her ambivalence, and I believe denial, was evident close to my birth. Six days before her due date, her water broke. The doctor told her to stay home until she felt contractions, the standard advice of the day. Three days later, she had significant abdominal pains but told my father she was having gas. My father was the one who insisted that she was in labor and that they go to the hospital. I was born that afternoon…to my father's relief, a girl with one head. I was a small, healthy baby, but not easy to comfort, at least not at first. According to my mother, I cried for five weeks pretty continuously before I settled down and became an easy child. She could not comfort me, but when my father held me I calmed right down. I was his "Dolly Dingle." Three weeks after my birth, my mother returned to work, and I was in the care of my father, who was in college, and Nanny, who now lived with us. They were loving, good caretakers, but they were not my mother.

My mother worked full-time all through my childhood, and for much of that time I felt her absence, despite the doting attention of my father and grandmother. Nonetheless, from an early age, I had disturbing, uncomfortable feelings about my mother that I could not articulate until I was in my late thirties. I sometimes described this as my mother "getting under my skin" for no clear reason, just a sensation. As a toddler and young child, I had skin discomfort from wool or any stiff fabric. My grandmother would take all the mesh crinolines out of my dresses and skirts so that I could wear them comfortably. I still am uncomfortable in most corduroy. There was no obvious skin condition, but I had goosebumps and a cringing sensitivity if such material touched my skin. To be enveloped by scratchy cloth felt like "fingernails on a blackboard." Perhaps this sense of my mother and my skin sensitivity harken back to those last days in her womb when there was no amniotic fluid…perhaps that environment became abrasive and the discomfort became associated with my mother as a person.

    I have almost no memories of close physical contact with my mother; rather, I recall longing for her. Nanny would take me and Tassie to the steps outside of our apartment building in Manhattan in the summer evenings to wait for my mother to return home from work. She would sing "She'll be Comin' 'Round the Mountain When She Comes" to pass the time, and I would fidget impatiently for my mother to appear. I do remember one physical activity that I enjoyed with my mother from toddlerhood. My mother would lie on her back on the bed with her legs up. She would place me across the soles of her feet, hold my hands, and move her legs, playing "Tree." As I looked into her eyes, the wind would blow (her legs would move from side to side) and I would excitedly anticipate the moment when the "tree" would fall (she would shift me onto the bed) and we would laugh. The thrill was in the danger of falling, of being let go. The laughter and excitement were relief that it was just a game.

    The awareness that became clear to me decades later was the sense that my mother would be very emotionally present, and then abruptly disappear. This was manifest overtly in her decision to return to work after only a few weeks caring for me, thus disrupting our attachment by her sudden absence. Yet her work-life was only a superficial expression of a much deeper wound; working might not have mattered if the underlying dynamic between us had been different. Even when physically present, my mother would leave me psychically. She would evaporate, and I would be left with longing. Not that she could not soothe me, rather that she could not stay with me emotionally. Just as I was beginning to rely upon her emotional presence, she would disappear, leaving a hole, a gap, a gulf. I could generate her attention, but I could not keep it. She might let go of me. The "tree" could fall at any moment. She might never come around the mountain/corner. Perhaps I cried for five weeks as a newborn not because my mother's closeness was toxic, but because her closeness was good…and then it was gone.

In the most pronounced form of connection and embodiment, in which Self and Other are at times indistinguishable—that of being inside a mother's womb/having a baby inside one's body—my mother was not consistently attentive to my presence. The lapses in her awareness of her pregnancy were paralleled after my birth in her lapses in comforting me and staying connected to me. Our mother-baby dyad became a separate mother and a separate baby too soon, too abruptly, too frequently. The dyad was not preserved; I could not keep her with me, no matter how much I wanted or needed her. My need for her carried no power. My mother's inadequacy in sustaining our interdependence created my sense of inadequacy for not being able to sustain her engagement. Her insecurity and discomfort with me created my insecurity and discomfort with her. The longing that was left was a chasm between us filled, for me, with the anger, loss, and self-loathing that are generated by a baby's helplessness in the face of a mother's withdrawal. This was the soil in which my deepest vulnerabilities found root.

In contrast, Bunny, despite his physical and emotional instability, was able emotionally to "hold" me more securely. On an external level, he may have been more at ease with infants, having been the second eldest of eleven children. Yet, on an interior level, he likely did not experience or communicate the same ambivalence that was present with my mother. He, and my grandmother, were able to sustain connection and comfort me, but the most essential bond, the bond with my mother, was forever weakened, ruptured. The resultant state of longing and loss marked most of my life.

My mother's psychic leavings, and the ambivalence in her that generated them, have branded all the major stresses in my life. Not the least of these were traumatic racial experiences that first manifested during my grade school years. Race and my bond with my mother may seem, at first glance, to be different issues, but in my life and my psychology their connecting strands run deep—as deep as my mother's unconscious feelings about bearing a child of mixed-race. The central dynamic of my mother's presence and absence might not have had the impact that it did on my psyche and my life were it not for the social experiences of my school years, and the school years might not have been so traumatic were it not for the ephemeral nature of my connection with my mother. If subsequent social connections in my childhood had offered more solace, the fractures between my mother and me might have had a chance to heal, but that was not to be the case.

I entered elementary school with advanced cognitive skills, overall emotional health, a compliant nature, and a basic assumption that others would like me. I adored my kindergarten and second-grade teachers and was comfortable with most of my other teachers as the years went on, but my first-grade teacher always seemed critical and angry with me and was impossible to please. Generally, rather shy and mild-tempered, I became withdrawn and unhappy in her classroom. From within my family and household, where racial issues were masked and muted, this teacher and the social texture of public school ripped off the mask, laying bare the animosity and divisiveness of race and class dynamics and the isolation of being deemed the Other. My experiences as a school-aged child also uncovered my mother's inability to offer emotional shelter around issues of race and codified certain unconscious feelings projected from her into destructive elements of my psyche. An Other-in-Self experience, her feelings embodied by me. The complexion of things had changed.

Throughout my early elementary school years, I had both white and black friends. My closest friend, Lynn, a chubby black child with dimples, is someone with whom I still have contact today. She is the youngest in a family of five children, and we spent many hours in each other's homes in addition to being in the same classes at school. We both played the flute and attended music school together for a number of summers. My closest white friend for many years was a girl from my dance class in a nearby suburb. A Jewish girl from an affluent family, Patty lived in a big state-of-the-art, split-level house with a large wooded area and stream behind it. I envied her house and the fancy neighborhood around it, but we played together well and enjoyed each other. We both played the piano, read a lot, and enjoyed schoolwork.

Other white friends came from my school and neighborhood. Italian girls of more middle-class means, they did not have fancy houses or property on which to play, but they were fun to "hang out with," and we rode bikes throughout our town together, freely and without helmets. Traffic was less intense then, and rules for kids and bikes were essentially non-existent. Race was not an issue in their company, and I felt comfortable and well-liked by them.

The black social community was harder to navigate than the white community. Signals about race were complicated and the terrain of race was treacherous. As a very light-skinned child with "good" hair, I was not clearly white or black. I was pretty, smart, and had parents with more financial resources than many of my black peers. I also had opportunities that were coded as "white," such as classical piano and modern dance lessons, a trip to France as a teenager, and frequent visits to New York City's cultural events. At first, I was just questioned by black children about my race. "Are you white or black?" But this expanded to become an interrogation of my blackness or black identity. "If you're black, let me see you dance." "Do you think you are better than me?" "You think you're cute because you have good hair!" The questions and comments became increasingly hostile and occasionally some group of black children would chase me home, calling me names and making threats.

By the third grade, I was frightened to go to school. Even though I was a good student and liked being with my friends, there was no protection offered from the adults around me, and my good school performance often aggravated the situation. I withdrew, began to read almost constantly, developed a series of nervous tics, such as blinking my eyes and biting my nails, and was overall rather lonely, depressed, and anxious. I did not comprehend the dynamics of envy or the rage that envy can generate, and there was no one to guide me. Every day I felt emotionally and physically at the mercy of others. To assuage feeling alone and vulnerable, I created imaginary (white) families, and I gave them imaginary names, homes, and interpersonal lives. My interior world was rich in these fantasied relationships, balancing my more troubled and meager external life. These fantasies suggest that I had the capacity for healthy, enriching human connections, a capacity that was stymied by the conflicts and hostility that weighed upon me. I believe that in those years, I unconsciously developed a less than straight posture that has been lasting—a bit slumped over—symbolically to bear emotional weight and to protect my heart.

My parents never knew of this. I never spoke to them of my struggles, and they did not pay attention. My mother lived in a denial about racial matters that rendered her oblivious to my distress, my father was not emotionally attuned to such things, and Nanny kept her feelings and observations about family matters to herself. With the exception of occasional conversations with Nanny, I did not confide in them about much of anything, let alone race. I behaved well, was a superior student, occupied myself, related to our dog, and did not rock the family boat.

My family existed with the premise that race did not matter. That was my parent's belief system, a core value shared in their marriage and their hope for the world. This world-view collided with my awareness that we were considered strange and worthy of suspicion. People stared at my family in public, sometimes rudely or with hostility. Occasionally, in a restaurant for example, when someone stared at us, my father would walk up to him or her holding onto his cane, extend his hand, and boldly introduce himself. That usually embarrassed, and perhaps chastened, the starer, but it also embarrassed me. As an adult, however, I admired him for that frankness.

For my mother, especially, a person's color was wholly unimportant, and she generally lived by this creed. Despite the racial intricacies in our relationship, she had the least ethnic, racial, or religious prejudice of anyone I have ever known. Helen held a lofty view of humankind and believed in goodness and the ultimate trajectory of moral right. This idealism, however, required a good bit of denial. My mother, oblivious to her pregnancy and to my imminent birth, also was oblivious to color and race. She never referred to people by race, even when it was quite obvious, and she never engaged in ethnic humor, stereotypes, or ethnic comments. She was politically correct well before it was politically correct to be politically correct! She also could not see the racial tension that I was experiencing socially, and I pretended that it did not exist. With this pretense, I colluded with her color-blindness, protected her from her inner Self, and preserved our tenuous bond. I was complicit in her denial.

My father was more direct in his approach to race, not engulfed in denial. He perceived racial tones in situations readily, and answered questions about race on forms with the response "Human." Any further distinction was not worth his attention. His color was not to be considered; only his humanity counted. He did not deny the significance of race, but he refused to succumb to the falsity and exaggeration of its true importance. Although Bunny was more realistic and aware about race, he was not particularly sophisticated in his understanding of emotions, and he did not handle strong affect comfortably; it distressed him. I did, however, sense that my father had an inkling of the racial pressures I was experiencing, but I also sensed that he did not have the capacity to address them.

Even though my disconnection from my mother left me feeling emotionally unprotected by her, she was a staunch advocate for me in outward ways. She kept my teachers on their toes about educational quality, she fought successfully with the city to create a public swimming pool, she always was on the lookout for interesting educational and cultural opportunities for me and was tireless in accessing them, and she shielded me from any unwarranted adult criticism. Yet, I never confided in my mother that I recall. Instead I recall a chilling threat of exposure at the prospect. I trusted her and her support, but not with my deepest, most private anxieties. In my mind, to preserve a tie with my mother, they had to be kept secret. One of the strains in being an only child in my circumstance was that no one around me had similar family or social experiences to mine. No one had the same complexion as me. No other children or adults, and neither of my parents. But I doubt that my mother ever considered that. She was color-blind.

I was ashamed, not of anything I did, but of who I was…ashamed that something was inherently defective about me, that I was "tainted"… a word that emerged in my psychoanalysis in my twenties and implies a darkening of color. I have thought that this term reflected my mother's unconscious feeling about me, one that I internalized but that did not originate with me. Rather, it became a part of me early in infancy as I absorbed my mother's unconscious affect, which generated and became inseparable from my melancholic tendencies. Perhaps my shame was really her shame. I also was ashamed that I had disappointed my parents in their belief that race was not important. In my mind, although probably not in theirs, I had failed to manage the racial landscape as they assumed I would, and I could not bring myself to let them know. By never mentioning any of the bullying, I spared them from their guilt and myself from the exposure of my failure, but I suffered greatly in my silence.

In elementary school, I developed solitary pursuits, particularly classical piano and reading. I also played the flute for a few years and went to summer music school for flute, but that was not as important in my life as books and piano. My piano life revolved around lessons from an unmarried, middle-aged Italian woman whose father was a violinist and classical pianist from Italy. He founded an elite music organization for young people that brought him and his daughter high regard throughout New Jersey for its excellence in music education.

My teacher and her parents, the Chiappinellis, lived in a very large white-elephant of a house with a wide porch and large rooms that contained probably six grand pianos. There was always a piano being played, students in and out, Italian spoken, and an atmosphere of music, music, music. There were lessons during the week and on the weekends, and through their music guild, there was an annual schedule of auditions, competitions, and Master Classes, and a sequence of performances for the competition winners, including a performance at Carnegie Hall.

Miss Chiappinelli was an excellent piano teacher, and I have been told in my later life by better pianists than me that I had very good training. She was passionate and intensely serious about music. She saw in me the beginnings of a serious professional pianist, and within a few years she wanted me to practice a minimum of four hours each day. I only did so very sporadically. Her expectations for me made me tense about lessons, and I fear that I disappointed her, which has never felt good. I guess that I had some talent for the piano, but classical piano study is difficult and requires dedication and immersion in extensive practice and study to excel beyond an intermediate level. A "B" level of expertise satisfied me, but not her. I enjoyed the piano, but I was not devoted to it.

Classical piano also was a very white and affluent vocation that definitely set me apart from my black classmates. My mother, who also played the piano (albeit to a lesser degree than me or certainly her sister), took me to state-wide piano competitions amidst almost solely white piano students usually from white affluent suburbs. These competitions were affiliated with my teacher's music organization and were stressful for me, always invoking the fears of failure and of disappointing her and my mother (inadequacy, defectiveness). We, piano students between the ages of six and eighteen, played a pre-selected music piece for a panel of judges, according to one's level of skill/experience, in a series of auditions that occurred every winter into the spring. The auditions were held at college campuses across the state, and the winner of the series of auditions for each level played at Carnegie Hall in Manhattan. Luckily, I never won the competition…I would have been paralyzed by anxiety in giving a formal performance in a prestigious concert hall.

I did, however, practice daily, reach an admirable level of accomplishment, and compete well. Nonetheless, like my Aunt Rosemary, I was not "the best." There was one other child of my age and musical level, a petit blond boy named Bobby, also a student of Miss Chiappinelli, who usually scored marginally better than me in these competitions. My musical nemesis. We were only casually friendly, but we were very aware of one another. His father held a major position with the state symphony orchestra and kept Bobby out of school every Friday for months to practice all day in preparation for these competitions. This, my mother told me, was the reason for his musical proficiency. "He is surrounded by music in his home and his life because of his father." I was surrounded by radical politics in mine. I saw this distinction as a sign of race and class difference and envied Bobby for his seeming ability to fit into the classical music upper-class white world so smoothly. He did, in time, make a career in music…not in classical piano but in composing music for theater and commercials. As I think back on it now, I guess I did have superior piano instruction if Bobby's parents, who had myriad classical music connections, chose Miss Chiappinelli to teach their son.

Although classical piano study brought me some esteem and pleasure, it was a lonely endeavor. Only my white friend, Patty, also played the piano. I recall one moment in the middle of my piano years when class and classical music clashed dramatically. My mother was playing our piano, which she did sometimes but not frequently. She played competently and pleasantly but not with any highly superior skill. At this particular time, I could not stand hearing it. I asked her, then begged her, to stop—it was painful to my ears. She did stop, but she was puzzled, not surprisingly, about what had happened. I could not answer—I did not know. I held my hands over my ears and ran into my room. Many years later, I understood vaguely that my reaction had something to do with whiteness and class, but I still cannot fully explain what had been stimulated in my psyche by hearing her play on that particular day.

After about seven or eight years, I abruptly abandoned my budding musical career. I fell in love with a young man and out of love with the piano. Scales and Beethoven could not compete with love and lust. I have since regretted ending my piano study, but I recognize that it was a casualty of my adolescence and of the relentless racial and class discord around me. I have played intermittently throughout my adulthood, and I own a lovely Steinway, but the piano carries with it memories about whiteness, blackness, class, and giving up that have made it hard to pursue piano music consistently. In my thirties during a spell of piano interest, but for no clear reason other than maybe nostalgia or closure of some sort, I phoned Miss Chiappinelli one Sunday morning. By then she was an elderly woman. Nevertheless, when she answered the phone, I heard someone beautifully playing a piano in the background, just like in the old days.

Miss Chiappinelli remembered me well and warmly and spoke to me of the talented "little Indian girl" to whom she was giving a lesson (on a Sunday morning!). She asked if I wanted her to teach my children, and I told her that I would if we still lived in New Jersey. I thanked her for her wonderful teaching over so many years, told her that I still enjoyed the piano, and commented that her little girl student was very fortunate to study with her. Miss Chiappinelli suggested that I learn a Debussy piece and then played a few bars of it for me. For a few moments, I was my ten-year-old piano Self once again, back in that large white house surrounded by classical music, with my teacher who had devoted her life to her love of classical piano.

By the age of eight, alongside my piano study, I read almost every moment that I could. I read at home, sitting outside, while walking down the street, on the bus. I could spend hours with a book. I spent a great deal of time in our local library, a different location than where my father worked. I identified with my father's love of books and reading, so libraries comforted me. For a year or two, I was engrossed in a children's book series called Freddy the Pig. I devoured every book in the twenty-six-book series, and as an adult I bought them all…they are on my bookshelf now and feel like familiars. Freddy was a pig who wore glasses and read newspapers, like my father. He also was head of the barnyard on Bean Farm, in which all the different animals generally got along well and had adventures together. How I wished it were so for me! Around the same age, I also looked to another member of the animal world for a strategy in relieving my conflicts. For a good while, I wanted a pet chameleon because my father told me that chameleons changed their color depending upon their environment. I was fascinated by this…how terrific that would be!! I did not get a chameleon as a child, nor did I buy one as an adult. That particular childhood craving did not withstand the test of time.

In the early 1960s, one was either white or black. Apart from being Chinese or perhaps Puerto Rican, there was no other option. To fit in among blacks, I had to persistently prove my blackness, which I had trouble doing. I often failed the tests, much to my humiliation. My ability to play classical piano or my knowledge of modern dance were not assets, nor was my intelligence. Being always at the top of the class and rewarded by teachers did not endear me among many of my classmates. This came to a peak in the sixth grade when our teacher was a 6'9" black man who had been a Harlem Globetrotter. He was the object of every student's desire for attention, but he knew my father, and I was clearly his pet student. Not a good thing! I was frequently taunted, but at moments that year I was despised.

From these experiences, I came to feel a heightened vulnerability around black peers that surfaced in anxiety, depression, and self-hatred. To fit in among whites, I had to ignore the fact that I had black roots, but that was easier than failing blackness tests. There was less envy, hostility, and humiliation, no overt threats, and my piano, modern dance skills, and intelligence counted. Either I was deemed to be a snooty, superior black despised by many other black children, or a blemished, inferior white who did not really belong. There was no bi-racial option. There was no term for bi-racial individuals then, other than then disparaging terms of "half-breed" and "mulatto." I was always the Other. In all my years of school, I knew three other children from parents who were interracially married, and two of them were siblings. In my high school of 2600 students, three of us were children from interracial marriages. There was no group anywhere with which to identify or to belong, and no siblings who shared the same fate. You were on your own, kid!

The longing that began with my mother, expanded into a longing for social acceptability and connection…to belong, to feel identified with someone like myself, not to feel different, and to recognize myself in others. At best, I was on the periphery of a group, not rejected but not fully welcomed. At worst, I was ostracized, humiliated, and threatened. I tried to live in the small space of friendship and safety amongst a few children that existed between fear of others and hatred of myself. Yet, I recall ways in which I was a kind and sensitive child to others.

Two examples of this have stayed with me. The first is my friend for a brief while, Alvin. Alvin was a boy in my neighborhood who wore braces on his legs, possibly from polio. He wanted to join the group of us who walked regularly to elementary school together, but the other children ran ahead, and he could not keep up with them. I stayed behind to walk with Alvin. I had some sympathy for people with disabilities. My other recollection concerns Sherry, a child near my age who had albinism and was mocked by other children for her very pale skin, odd eyes, and strange straw-colored hair. At a high school reunion in the 1980s, Sherry approached me to thank me for being so kind to her. She said that I was the only child in the neighborhood who had been friendly to her. I told her that I was glad that I had been kind to her, and that I appreciated her comment. I guess that I also had sympathy for children with issues around skin color.

To feel included and connected, I wished to have a common name, like Susan, or Cathy, or Debbie. The name Naomi, which I grew to like as an adult, was very weird when I was a child, and it signaled my difference. I longed to dress like other girls, but my mother bought clothes from expensive department stores in Manhattan, whereas my peers shopped at cheaper stores, like Sears along the highway. My clothes were nicer, but no one else had clothes like them, and I was again, different and strange. My mother inculcated in me a streak of her own "New York City class elitism," which existed quietly within a corner of her personality. I enjoyed this as an adult, but it was disastrous in my childhood.

I had entered school a year early because of my early January birthday and my strong cognitive skills, so I was younger than the other children in my class. At my sixth grade graduation, all the girls wore the newest item… pantyhose! My mother did not think that it was appropriate for a girl of my age to wear "stockings," so she forced me to wear knee socks with my dress. I was mortified!! She also subjected me to public humiliation when I won a citizenship award in late elementary school. There was a ceremony in which we were asked to take a Loyalty Oath. My mother's hackles were up! She walked up on the stage, physically removed me, commenting to the principal on the stage that no child should be taking an oath to anything, particularly a political oath! Again, with good intentions, she totally missed my need not to be different in favor of her own ideology.

My father's drinking separated me from others as well. The fathers of many children drank…it was a sign of the times. Yet, my father was particularly vociferous when intoxicated, and everyone knew he had an alcohol problem. I was in total conflict about this. I loved him, was angry and ashamed of him, was embarrassed by him, and then felt guilty for my shame and embarrassment. I did not understand the link between his drinking and his physical and emotional pain, so I could not feel the compassion for him that might have tempered my embarrassment. I was not comfortable with who he was when drinking, or who I was in reference to him.

Similar conflict, shame, and distress were acute even without the element of alcohol when my father brought me to my modern dance class in the nearby affluent suburb in which my friend, Patty, lived. She and I met in this dance class. The weekly class was held on the stage of a school auditorium, and my father had to walk down the aisle for me to join the class. My older father with his bald head, brown skin, and cane walked slowly and awkwardly, and everyone stared.

They seemed to be shocked and confused having seen me on other days accompanied by my (white) grandmother. As my mother worked on Saturday mornings, she never brought me to class. I was unlike all the other girls whose mothers did not work and were always present, and whose fathers and grandmothers were never seen.

On an individual level, with the exception of the black peers that threatened me, people liked me pretty well. I did make and keep friends, but I never melded with any group until my graduate school years when I bonded with others around psychoanalysis. For those years, I was socially active and felt connected to others like me because we were all immersed in psychoanalysis. Otherwise, I lived as the "Other," and my family reflected my Otherness and difference.

The essence of such experiences has instilled in me recurrent themes throughout my life. Always my deep relationships have been solely on an individual basis. I am a good friend and parent and I have close friendships of forty years, but I do not have identifications with race, religion, ethnicity, or any other group. I eschew groups and gatherings because I find them potentially too dangerous and destructive, and I will not participate in experiential groups of any kind. I can socialize perfectly smoothly, but I do not join things or entertain others very often. Commonplace forms of socialization are not pleasurable for me.

Reflecting the repeated psychic loss in my evanescent bond with my mother, my natural mood has remained at the slightly depressed side of normal, punctuated by periods of happiness, periods of acute anxiety, and a few spells of deeper depression. Feelings of connection brighten and fade. The glass is still half-empty, and I still expect the tunnel at the end of the light. My father's comments on the balance between pleasure and insult, licks and kisses, embraces and being spit upon perhaps foretold this perspective of mine. His emotional wounds and his reflections upon them, internalized by me, became mine. The transmission of generational trauma. In the most recent decade of my life, I have become more misanthropic and reclusive, but this is where I feel safest and least vulnerable. Solitude brings its comforts and protections.

I have wondered if my childhood would have been easier if my parents had found a therapist for me. However, there were far fewer therapists at that time than now, most were white male psychiatrists, and the culture did not support child psychotherapy as it does currently. As I thought this idea through, I realized that the chance of finding a therapist in the 1960s that understood my racial dilemma was slim to none. A few years ago, I read an article about a female psychiatrist, the first black woman to complete psychoanalytic training in New York City. She had recently died but had practiced actively in the 1960s. To my surprise, the article mentioned that she had specialized in an unusual field… children with psychological issues around race! Perhaps therapy with her might have altered things for me, but who knew?

In my school-aged years, a cultural groundswell was unfolding. The second phase of the Great Migration was changing the racial landscape of the country. In US history, the Great Migration occurred between 1916-1970, bringing six million blacks from the rural South to the cities of the North and West. The first migration began as European emigration to the US waned during World War I, only to surge again at the end of World War II. As Isabel Wilkerson details so well in her wonderful book on this arduous migration, "*The Warmth of Other Suns*," the blacks who escaped the violence, poverty, and Jim Crow laws of the segregated South to seek better social and economic conditions had abilities that not all blacks enjoyed.

Among these abilities were strong intelligence, the capacity to make and execute plans in secret, skills that would be transferable to a new environment and a new type of labor, self-restraint and courage, hope and fortitude. People without these attributes could not make this journey. The travelers left behind many of the infirm, the elderly, those with cognitive or emotional deficits, or those who were too afraid to leave. They traveled by train at night to destinations in the North, usually settling in cities with train service or joining family who had already settled there. New York, Chicago, Philadelphia, Detroit, Baltimore, Los Angeles were common destinations. However, well before Wilkerson composed her thoughts on paper, my father said: "The smart Negroes left [the South]…got the hell out. The others had babies and had to eke out a living to support them." There were now faint fracture lines dividing Northern and Southern blacks in the cohesion of the Black Experience.

In many ways, this venture North was disappointing. New stresses abounded. Those who left were separated from family, friends, community to make a new life in an unfamiliar environment. Farming and labor skills appropriate to a rural environment had to be exchanged quickly for skills in industry, as homes isolated in the countryside were exchanged for apartment dwellings in large cities. Although blacks escaped the confines and injustice of Jim Crow laws and legal segregation and had the possibility of economic growth and stability, discrimination was rampant in the North as well. Blacks were segregated into ghetto communities, and Northern blacks tended to look down upon the rural Southern blacks. The clear, immovable social and legal boundaries of the South gave way to murky and confusing rules and expectations in the North.

Socialization between whites and blacks was permitted in the North, but the rules and boundaries were mercurial, situational, and often covert.

Southern blacks who were totally clear about Southern race rules could not negotiate the new subtleties easily. The Southerners were resented by the European immigrants who came before them and whose jobs they now threatened, a similar refrain to that heard in current immigration issues. The urban environment, noise, and cold weather, as opposed to the simpler, quieter, and warmer rural countryside of the southern states could feel oppressive. The constant stark fear endemic to segregation was replaced by the chronic, grinding anxiety of the unfamiliar and uncertain.

Many of the first generation of Southerners in the North were dismayed, and individuals did not necessarily do well. It was the second generation that reaped the benefits of their predecessors' effort and sacrifice to achieve better education, better living and work conditions, and more equality. Demographics have shifted since 1970, with more blacks returning to the South as air conditioning, better work environments with better pay, less racial discrimination now exist, but the trend of black Southerners heading North has not been reversed. Old attitudes about Northern and Southern blacks are still present.

By the mid-1960s, this second migration was well underway. Black children from the rural South entered my neighborhood and elementary school in noticeable numbers. The newcomers were friendly, approachable, and ultimately welcomed, but they brought noticeable cultural differences. Because of the short academic year in the South due to the timing of sowing and harvesting crops, and the segregated inferior education of black children, black students were automatically placed in a grade below their stated grade. Often they had strong southern accents, unusual habits such as combing their hair on their front steps, different food preferences, and they were not as socially or verbally facile as the Northern children. Because of being "put behind a grade," as it was termed, my classmates from the South tended to be bigger and more physically developed than my northern peers.

Despite these differences, the southern black children assimilated into the social alliances already established, but many were less comfortable around me than were their northern counterparts. They seldom seemed at ease in my home with my interracial parents and white grandmother.

One of my black southern classmates was meek and timid around my family, and totally surprised that she could use our bathroom or share a snack with me. The father of another child in my neighborhood, a very large man with a big deep voice and six children, became distinctly nervous and subservient in the presence of my small, mild-tempered mother. I registered his anxious energy, but I did not understand it until years later. No matter that my mother was gentle and kind, he harbored a fear of the power of her whiteness.

I absorbed a lot about "black culture" in those years that I realized as an adult most white people do not understand. I learned the depth of the prejudice within the black community around skin color, hair texture, language inflection. I experienced first-hand the envy and distrust that existed between darker-skinned and lighter-skinned blacks, blacks with "good hair" and blacks with "nappy hair." I learned the importance of loud humor and strong emotion among loved ones as a respite and release from daily stress and trouble. I saw the personal and cultural shame around being black that permeated the black community, and the contempt and derision that whites knowingly and unknowingly extended.

Color discrimination among blacks is rooted in slavery, during which many lighter-skinned blacks had the chance to live in the "Big House" and work indoors away from the sun. Some of them were given secret opportunities to read or learn, to travel, or to make some relationship with whites. They were not treated at all equal to whites—they were still enslaved and considered inferior—but life was a bit easier. Darker-skinned blacks often spent their years in the fields, subject to harder physical labor and the effects of relentless heat and humidity. Among the descendants of those enslaved, being dark of skin color continued to be a source of great self-hatred and humiliation. This has not been forgotten in cultural memory. As the saying went: "If you're white, you're right; if you're yellow, you're mellow; if you're brown, stick around; if you're black, git back."

I remember distinctly the efforts of my black friends' mothers to "press" their hair with oil and an iron in an arduous time-consuming process in the attempt to make their hair look more like white people's hair…or more like mine. I remember the jokes made by blacks about black physical and psychological characteristics that served to degrade and shame themselves, and I remember feeling guiltily relieved that those terms did not usually apply to me. Later, when Barack Obama was elected to the presidency, I noted that his daughters were introduced to the public with straightened hair ("relaxed" in today's terminology), looking as "white" as possible. Probably wise in terms of his electability, but rather sad to see. In recent days, Michelle Obama publicly confided her unwillingness to keep her hair "natural" during her years in the White House, feeling the need to keep it straight and smooth, rather than curly and loose. (Washington Post, Nov. 17, 2022).

Many black families in the 1960s were much like white families in structure. Most of my peers had two parents in the home, with perhaps an extended relative, but living habits differed. Not all black families were alike, of course, but I observed some generalities that were different from my family and from the families of my white friends. In many black homes, children had a definite "place" in the family, one unequal to the role of adults and with little power or room to express themselves. The father of one friend of mine would say to us sternly: "The grownups are talking…disappear!!!" Feelings were not too important, but behavior was. Fathers tended to be strict and authoritarian, mothers deferred to male authority, and children were to be quiet and obedient.

As children became young teenagers, daughters had extensive family responsibilities in areas of child care, domestic tasks, catering to immediate wishes of the parents for a snack or to be brought something. "Please" and "thank you" usually were not included in such requests. Sons were given more freedom, and their needs superseded those of their sisters. Suspicion of outsiders was often active, and education and childhood friendships were not always valued. Whereas my house was full of reading material of all kinds, books were seldom in evidence in their homes, and my only "chore" was to succeed in school. Some of these characteristics were present in the families of my white friends as well, but they seemed much more pronounced among the families of my black friends. A certain ease, informality, and casualness was felt between parents and children in the white families that I encountered that was harder to find in black households. Black children seemed to be prepared early for the daily responsibilities of adult life.

I became aware of the roots of these patterns and of certain stereotypes, such as blacks owning large cars like Cadillacs and Oldsmobiles, and bringing lots of food to outings, in the experience of Southern white prejudice. Large cars were needed to drive from the North to the South to visit family because there was no guarantee that one would be able to find food or a place to sleep below the Mason-Dixon line. Having sleeping room and enough food for a family in one's car was a necessity. In families with limited material comforts, food, humor, protection, which sometimes defined love, were paramount. Such adaptations were formed by necessity and resilience and reflected healthy pragmatic strategies for preserving safety and quality of life.

I learned from my father and an aunt that the quick physical punishment that was common among black families was at its origins not abuse, but protection. In the South before Civil Rights laws were enacted and enforced, a young black child had to learn to respond immediately to white privilege and authority. To be deferential, obedient, subservient, and not to assert himself or herself in any way, especially not in anger, was critical for safety and survival. No talking back, no arguing, no expressing your opinions or feelings, no jokes. If a white person said something, you obeyed immediately with your eyes lowered and your temper under full control. This was learned best and earliest in the home. Hence, in reference to a sometimes harsh spanking, the phrases "I'm doing this for you" and "I brought you into this world and I will take you out." My parents encouraged opinions and some dissent, had discussions with me about my behavior, and did not spank. In contrast, the parents, particularly the fathers, of many of my black peers were strict disciplinarians, no nonsense, quick to use a belt on the buttocks. Love was around without question, but unyielding discipline was too. Sometimes the two were hard to distinguish, at least for those who were unfamiliar with all the signals. In terms of culture, old habits die hard.

Although prejudice was reflected in my social experiences as a child, I recall only one experience of frank discrimination. When I was about nine, my parents took me to Palisades Amusement Park with a largely black bus group that left from Newark. We had a good day, and at the end of the day I wanted to swim in the pool there. My father approached the pool area and was immediately turned away because "Negroes cannot swim here." He reached down and explained that to me, but I did not understand, and I probably whined. I could see that he was upset. I imagine now that he felt angry, helpless, and humiliated. After awhile, we left the park and returned to the bus, which was scheduled to leave at 7:00. But the bus didn't move at 7:00 or soon thereafter, even as other buses that arrived after us left.

My father approached the bus driver and remarked that other buses had left. "Why are we still here?" The bus driver responded that he could not leave until the bus was full, which was not the case with the other buses. My father sat back down. A long time passed, darkness fell, and I could see that my father was getting angrier. Without a comment, he went back to the bus driver, leaned into him and said, "The bus is leaving now." The bus driver pulled away and we rode home. The next day I gleaned from an angry conversation between my parents, and years later was told by my mother, that my father had pulled a small knife from his pocket and pressed it against the driver's side.

My father was not aggressive, and I do not think he was planning to actually stab this man, but he was angered and humiliated by the prejudice expressed at the swimming pool and again at the bus stop, and he needed to reestablish a sense of worth and power. My mother was furious with him, stating that he put his family in jeopardy. What if he had been arrested, or what if the driver had responded violently? My father, after all, was handicapped and not fit for a physical fight.

This was the only time in my life that I saw my mother truly angry or my parents fighting bitterly. My mother threw the knife away and insisted that my father seek psychological help.

Reluctantly, my father agreed. He would only go to the VA for treatment, as he considered treatment his due for his war service, so he went to the nearby VA Hospital. He saw a psychiatrist once who focused solely on his alcohol use. My father told the doctor that he did drink a lot but that he worked steadily, did not run with other women, did not abuse his wife or child, or misuse money. That he liked to drink and when he wanted to stop, he would. Otherwise, he planned to continue drinking. So much for rehab! The doctor apparently did not address my father's traumas at the origin of his alcoholism. My father did continue to drink for at least another ten years, but he stopped abruptly after being sick one morning following a binge, telling my mother that he was just too old to continue drinking. He never drank again for the remaining decades of his life, although he did become depressed.

As my personal racial conflicts were unfolding, the country was undergoing radical cultural and societal changes. The Vietnam War was escalating and the Civil Rights Movement was making headway into established patterns of racial discrimination. By the time I was around twelve, the tide was turning culturally, but major changes occurred closer to home. My grandmother, who had lived with us all my life, left our home to live with her younger sister, Frances, after the death of her older sister, Minnie. Frances, who never married and had taught kindergarten, had lived much of her adult life with Minnie, who threw her husband out of their home after six weeks of marriage. Their home in Missouri was very near the home in which my mother and Rosemary grew up.

When Minnie died, Frances came to New Jersey and found an apartment in our town with my grandmother. I saw my grandmother some afternoons after my school day and every Sunday after she went to church, but it was not the same as having her in the same house. Also that summer, Tassie, our dear family dog, died at sixteen, which was very sad for all of us, and my Uncle Max died suddenly. I lost my grandmother's constant presence…she who "saved me" from the wind, from the door closing on me, from my father's intoxicated tirades, and from the full impact of my mother's emotional and physical absences. Tassie's death took away a special friend, one who was also "saved" by my grandmother. My uncle's death brought grief to my mother and grandmother, which did not go unnoticed by me.

In a time when children were allowed to roam their neighborhoods freely, I began to develop a private life separate from my parents. You know, that life of secrecy and subterfuge often emerging in early-mid adolescence. I spent parts of that summer at a sleep-away camp that I loved, attended music school, and enjoyed a group of white friends. We rode bikes, went horseback riding, and just talked and listened to rock-and-roll. But I also explored other worlds unbeknownst to my parents.

My girlfriends and I would leave our homes after breakfast and return for dinner with no acknowledgement of where we were going or where we had been. Parents seldom asked, and we did not always know ahead of time. We wandered as the spirit moved us, on foot, on our bikes, by bus. A good bit of the time we hung out in a local park, at a bowling alley miles away, or threw water balloons from the balcony of the penthouse of one of my friends, or just walked around eating ice cream or sticky buns and listening to music. My father would comment on his mixed feelings seeing me ride off on my bike with my white friends whose "long hair blew in the wind."

I struggled with choosing "white" music like the Beatles, the Beach Boys, Simon and Garfunkel, the Rolling Stones, the Byrds, Bob Dylan to which I listened with my white friends, or the black "Motown Sound" and "Philadelphia Soul" of the Supremes, the Temptations, the Jackson 5, Gladys Knight, Smokey Robinson, the Stylistics, the Moments, the Delfonics, the Intruders that were dominating the black music scene and the black community in the mid-late 60s.

As much as I loved soul music, I could not dance well…or at least not in comparison to black children. Years of modern dance classes did not quite foster the fluid shoulder and hip movements, or the rhythms and fast footwork that my black peers did so easily. Nor did my family life include years of soul music always playing in the background as was often the case in their homes. The sounds of classical piano at the Chiappinellis or my father's favorite tunes did not cut it. I was frequently mocked and humiliated for my awkward dance movements, a source of great personal shame that lifted a bit only in my early adulthood. Then, amongst white peers, I was frequently complimented on my dancing, and to my surprise I WAS better than them!

In the early years of Motown, almost no "black music" was played on white radio stations. Black teenagers listened to black radio and white radio, but white teenagers seldom even knew that black radio stations existed. After perhaps Elvis and a few other artists, Motown performers were among the first to cross the racial barrier in music, radio, and popular culture, but that took time to become commonplace. And there were many more black groups and soloists beyond the most prominent ones popular with white listeners. I had to keep my appreciation of white music secret around my black friends and hide my interest in Motown around my white friends. I had to keep current with the black music world in order to pass blackness tests, but I could not let my white friends know that I listened to black radio stations. No biracial music around. While many "things black" have gone from my life, my favorite music is still the artists of Motown and the Philadelphia Sound from the mid-60s and early 70s. The best music ever!

Also that summer for reasons that should seem clear, I became a bit obsessed with birth and death. I walked to the local hospital and asked unsuccessfully to see a dead body, and I ventured a few times to the maternity floor to look at newborn infants. Obviously, this was before hospitals had any serious security. My interest in death was connected to the loss of Tassie, the sudden death of my Uncle Max, and the absence of my grandmother at home, all within a few weeks' time, but a few other aspects of that summer are relevant to my curiosity about babies.

The teenaged daughter of a neighbor, who I considered a friend although she was four years older than me, became pregnant. As I got older, I realized that she used me as a guise for having sexual liaisons with a number of young men and was promiscuous, if not actually a prostitute. But I liked Karen, and she liked me. We would spend weekend afternoons together walking to the house of one of these men, she would go into a back room with one for awhile, and then we would walk home. I had no idea what they were doing. I would spend that time in the living room, sometimes all by myself or sometimes with some random family member of Karen's "friend."

Often their homes were strange to me…dark with curtains drawn, no books, no adults around, no social etiquette, sometimes with toddlers wandering around aimlessly by themselves. Another cultural experience! Karen's parents sent her to the South suddenly and secretively for the duration of her pregnancy, and she returned with a baby girl. Unwed teen pregnancy was shameful in the black and the white communities of the time, but black families seemed less quick to force marriage or to cast out their daughters permanently. When all was said and done, when the baby arrived, black families usually rose to the occasion, embraced the babies and their daughters, and did their best to care for them.

For a year or two starting that summer, I had a secret relationship with a white boy my age who had long white-blond hair and blue eyes. Jay lived with his mother and sister in an apartment, but his mother was never home during the day. I had my first sexual experiences with him in his apartment…not intercourse, but kissing, touching, and experiencing sexual feelings. He was a friend of my girlfriends as well, and he sometimes would chase us around his apartment with a knife playfully as a joke. Although his behavior was in actuality more dangerous than what I faced from the black children at school, it was less frightening because it was not accompanied by hostility and menace. We laughed and screamed with silliness. Although it was mildly disconcerting at the time, it appalled me as an adult. My parents did not know about Jay… they would never have allowed me to see him had they known.

Additionally, another white friend, Linda, and I bonded that summer, sharing encounters with a grown man and his attempts to seduce us. She lived in an apartment across from an office building with her mother, her stepfather who was a police officer, and her baby brother. Her mother was quite overweight and, even to my young perception, unhappy and overwrought. We were always taking her baby brother with us in our wanderings because her mother wanted him out of the house. We did our best to care for him properly, and I often enjoyed his babyishness and my "mothering" role, although Linda found it less gratifying. She probably did it all day. Amidst our attentions, the baby was dragged into less than ideal situations, fed randomly, and spent most of the time in his stroller. After all, we were only twelve!

That summer, a man in the office building across from Linda's apartment building took a hankering to her, more than to me, but tried to get both of us to come to his house and later offered to take us on a cruise. Linda was sorely tempted to go to his home, but I refused, and she would not go without me. I felt safe from this man because I was clear and confident that I was never going to spend time with him. I sensed that something was wrong with him, a sensibility that Linda did not have.

Linda was repeatedly making connections with grown women of questionable circumstances who had babies or toddlers. One of these women had a niece who was twelve years old and pregnant, which shocked me. She was my age!! I did not understand that she had probably been raped by one of the many men who came through that household. Linda's stepfather was also worrisome. He was sexually inappropriate with us and probably molested my friend. He would "goose" us as we passed by him and give us seductive looks. Later in her adolescence when we were no longer close, Linda sadly became addicted to heroin. This was an era of childhood freedom and exploration with minimal adult supervision. Parents did not hover, and children were free to create parent-free worlds. A wonderful sense of liberty and autonomy came about, with opportunities to make decisions and judgments independent of adult input, but there were ever-present dangers.

In contrast to being afraid of black girls on a daily basis, only one time did I ever feel fear in the presence of whites. Around the age of nine, I attended a July 4th celebration with my parents at the library in which my father worked. I was very familiar with the building, having spent time there with my father, and when I had to use the bathroom I felt comfortable going by myself. When I entered the restroom that day, there were only two other girls there, teenagers sitting on the sink counter smoking. As I left the toilet stall, they jumped down from the counter and encircled me, taunting me about what I had done in the toilet, and if I was "a good little girl," and they made it difficult for me to leave. I was too intimidated and frightened to say anything, but after a few minutes they let me go.

My black and white friends almost never intersected. I am not sure if they ever knew each other, except for my dance friend Patty who had met Lynn. Whites and blacks rarely integrated socially. In the outer world, legal segregation was eliminated, but de facto separation, discrimination, and bigotry still permeated society and culture. In some ways, the country was moving in a good direction in terms of racial issues, but this came with more difficult times for me as Black Power arrived. Instead of my light skin and "good hair" being a desirable, albeit envied, trait within the black community, among many it now marked me as "white" and as a traitor to my black heritage.

The cultural shift toward pride in being black now allowed hatred and resentment of "whiteness" and its variants, which may have been a long-standing cultural undercurrent among blacks, now to be openly expressed and validated. Hostility brewed amongst black peers whom I had considered friendly acquaintances, and their anger found its way to me. "Are you black or are you white?" In order to be accepted, I was expected to denounce my whiteness and claim only my blackness, which equated to denouncing my mother. Another blackness test! When I would not do that, I was ostracized and belittled. School became an even more frightening place.

One of my good friends from school joined the Black Muslims, along with many other students, and totally disparaged whites. She later moved away from that position and told me that her change of heart was partly generated by her memory of my mother as being kind and decent. Her husband, who she married right after high school and with whom she had two children, also changed his mind about the Nation of Islam. He had an affair with a white woman and left my friend to pursue this relationship.

In this same time period of the late 1960s, the country erupted into racial riots. One of those riots occurred in Newark, New Jersey, the large city adjacent to my town. My parents and others were frightened of the nearby violence, and everything felt unsettled and on-edge. Within one year of the riots, my high school of 2600 students, which had been well-integrated, became almost totally black after almost all the white families moved to the western suburbs and new black families moved in from Newark. White flight at its best! The remaining white students, of which there may have been fifty, banded together in a few small social cliques, separated from the surrounding black student population. It became more and more difficult to have both black and white friends.

My parents considered moving as well but did not do so. Their ideology led them to the position that leaving was the path by which ghetto neighborhoods were created. (True!) When the stable families leave, the problems escalate, and they did not want to participate in that trajectory. So we stayed. My immediate neighborhood remained solid and safe enough, but the surrounding city deteriorated rapidly as the more stable and financially sound families made a rapid escape, and poorer families from Newark arrived, leaving the city open to the urban ills of the time. It was a sad transition that pains me even today when I think about it.

I wonder: if my parents had known about the racial stress that I endured at school, would they have made the same choice? They did consider the prospect of sending me to private school, but there was only one private school possible, and that school was an hour's bus ride away. Due to my father's drinking, my mother wisely refused to have a car in the household, so we managed with public transportation. This was not too difficult usually, as buses were convenient and accessible, but it was difficult to move within the suburbs. If I went to that private school, I would be in an all-white social situation fairly far from home. The distance would limit my participation in school activities, and I would not be readily able to socialize outside of school with my classmates. Their families would be much more affluent, and I would be the Other for reasons of both race and class. Private schools in the 1960s were the bastion of the wealthy. A Catholic school was a more local option, but my mother refused to have me educated in Catholicism. The days of mid-range secular and religious private schools were yet to come. They were ushered in by resistance against school integration and by the movement to the suburbs that was just beginning.

So for the last few years of high school, I remained in a largely black, poorer environment than when I started school, suddenly exposed to social discord and distress on a scale that I had not known before. The highly rated school system that we moved from New York City to access was now a thing of the past. For example, whereas in my first two years of high school, students could choose to take French, Spanish, German, Italian, Spanish, or Latin for at least two years, by my last year Spanish was the only alternative. I do not know the statistics, but in my memories of high school, the increase in unwed pregnancy, drug use, and violence was dramatic. Interest in academics declined as did respect for good academic performance. Being a good student was ridiculed.

One of my classmates who became pregnant was "sent away" for "lung treatment" returning with a baby. Another got married at fifteen and pregnant. A few others were known to have had babies who were raised as their siblings or in the homes of "aunts" living nearby. "Aunt" or "auntie" often meant their mother's closest friends. As my father's family exemplified, adoption among black families was often informal and was a generic, rather than literal or legal, term. Similar references to "cousins" might also reference close peers rather than actual cousins. ("Cousin" is a term also used in parts of Africa currently to describe close childhood peers, as children often spend more time with their peers than with adult family members.)

In Health (Sex Education) class, I sat in front of a sixteen-year-old (admitted) prostitute who had a "trick baby." She made learning about menstruation, breast development, and intercourse seem rather quaint. There was a sophomore who bore a baby in the school bathroom, alone by herself. Eventually, the school district instituted a special program for pregnant teens, and these girls left regular school early in their pregnancies. We also had a white teacher almost killed by students who soaped the bathroom floor and then called her in on false pretense of helping them. She promptly fell and hit her head badly on the slippery tile. There were incidents of violent abuse and threats toward the white students. Drugs were starting to creep around the corners. In those years, to me, these incidents were nothing less than shocking, and they inspired fear, dread, and confusion. To some degree, my parents were aware of the social changes, but the usual family dynamic applied. My mother was oblivious to the impact of these changes on me, my father was unsure of how or whether to address them and just didn't, and I did not acknowledge any problem. The family myth that race doesn't matter was sustained.

One of my friends in adolescence presented a different racial and class distinction than is usual. Marcy was a slender, pretty, and smart black girl with a light complexion. Marcy belonged to the "Black Bourgeoisie," a class of well-to-do blacks with a long tradition of upper-class social conventions. Originally from the South with Atlanta, Georgia as a center of activity in the 1960s, the black families in this class stratum were the families of physicians, lawyers, successful businessmen, celebrities, and other professionals. Many of the black bourgeoisie originated among the blacks descended from "house slaves," who had opportunities to rub elbows with the white world and sometimes to share ancestry with white slave owners. Many of them had white or mixed-race members somewhere in their family lineage and many had light complexions. In fact, light complexions were valued as a sign of status.

The families in this social stratum achieved the money and trappings of the white affluent classes, and developed lifestyles concerned with status and conspicuous consumption. They mimicked the white upper-class by giving cotillions, debutante balls, coming-out parties. Detached from the traditional black world and never fully accepted as equal to whites despite their lifestyle similarities, the black bourgeoisie orbited in its own sphere with its own social codes. Image and status were highly important. Sometimes, the members of this elite group were the butt of jokes, envy, and derision by other blacks who viewed them as "uppity," but more often they looked down upon other blacks, considering them to be inferior. The black bourgeoisie had its heyday in the 1940s-1970s but remained relevant long after that time. Its members were influential in the establishment of Historic Black Colleges and Universities

(HBCUs), civic and charitable organizations, and in black communities in large cities all across the country.

Despite her "superior" social background, Marcy was struggling with personal trauma and troubles. She had come to my school as a young teenager from another state after her mother's death under suspicious circumstances. Marcy and her father and siblings left their community partly to avoid the humiliation that public awareness of her mother's death brought upon the family. They lived with a relative in a large house, and Marcy socialized with other members of elite black social organizations. Her mother had been a very light-skinned black woman from an affluent black family, and it was Marcy's brother who found her dead mother's body. Marcy did not reveal details of her mother's death to me until a few years after we met. Her cover story was that her mother died of a medical condition, which was technically true, but evaded the most powerful piece of this event.

Marcy lived her life on a class boundary within the black community. She socialized both among the more middle-class teenagers in our school and the black elite from elsewhere. She traveled regularly by plane to Atlanta, which was unusual for those days, she attended cotillions and dances among the black bourgeoisie, and she interacted with other often affluent blacks from neighboring communities. She was a member of the "Jack and Jill Club," a civic and social organization restricted to monied blacks that promoted events for the young black bourgeoisie. Despite her upper-class affiliation and its white trappings, Marcy was not treated as hostilely and aggressively as me. Envy toward her did not erupt into hatred because she did not have a white parent; she was not viewed as a "traitor to her race."

At the other end of the spectrum was the cohort group of malevolent girls who despised me. Two sisters who came from a poor family and were raised without their biological parents were particularly bitter and malicious. The younger of the sisters was very short and had a body deformity, which the older one did not. The younger one was the more vicious and militant of the two, but they both stalked me and regularly threatened to "beat me up" and to "get me after school" for a year or two. Twice, they accosted me outside of school, and I barely escaped confrontation. Once I quickly ran out of a store when I saw them come in, glaring at me, and another time an adult passer-by broke up what was to be an assault. Luckily, in those years, there were no weapons. In retrospect, I recognize that these girls were probably abused in their own homes, possibly lived within the foster care system, and suffered with significant cognitive and emotional dysfunction. At that time, however, they were just scary.

In the absence of any parental guidance or understanding, my own skills and defenses had to suffice. I dealt with the sea change in my environment wrought by the "white flight" in the wake of the riots with increased anxiety, but also with a social strategy that was not fully deliberate, but rather resourceful. I was in mostly Honors classes with some white students and some black students, all of whom were relatively solid and well-adjusted. Our homeroom, Health, Home Education, and gym classes, however, were with everyone, including the pregnant, violent, and disturbed members of the student population.

Each year I made some friendly connection with one or two of the more stable black girls in one of those classes. I did not socialize with them outside of school, but we were friendly in school. My affiliation with them was a bulwark against some of the hostility and aggression from some of the other students. These girls were not among the Honor students, the wealthier students, or the white students, but, even if not popular, they were accepted. They offered a "safe zone" between the white students, the small number of academically successful students with whom I was most friendly, and the angrier, more aggressive contingent of other students. I felt that they "had my back," at least a bit, a comfort in the absence of my parents.

The other element in my life that allowed me to survive emotionally was the romantic relationship that I developed at a very young age. In the summer between my freshman and sophomore years of high school, a black family with two sons moved across the street from me. The younger boy was my age, and we started a friendship. One day when we were sitting on his porch, his older brother came outside with us, a handsome young man with olive skin and black curly hair who was attending a local college. He sat with us for awhile, and when I went back across the street to my house I was a different girl. Steven, who my father came to call Estebanico, and I fell in love to romantic tunes from Detroit and Philly and developed a serious intimate relationship that lasted ten years.

When I returned to high school that fall, I was full of romantic ideas and feelings, and I had a new repository for my emotions and longings. As the year went by, Steven and I spent more and more time together, and it became a habit for him to drive me to school and sometimes pick me up. My involvement with a handsome college student was a feather in my cap socially, his presence was a barrier to overt confrontations, and the hostility toward me became less frequent. He was six years older than me and seemed very knowledgeable and sophisticated at the time. At that age, I was sweet, accommodating, naive, and somewhat dependent, and for many of our first years together the sun rose or set in his eyes.

My parents were welcoming to Steven, extending fondness and full acceptance of him in my life. He and I were attached at the hip, and he spent a great deal of time with my family as well as with me. His family was stable and middle-class, although his parents were far less educated than mine. I also met my father's mandate in being with Steven, a mandate expressed only when my father was intoxicated and partly, but only partly, as a joke: "Don't bring any boy home who is darker than me." Unconsciously, Steven and I solved racial dilemmas for each other. He was often mistaken for Puerto Rican because of his skin color and hair texture. He was black, but different from many black men of his age in his appearance, mannerisms, and attitudes. He went to a largely white college and seemed to have identified with white more than black culture.

We engaged in a lot of sex but were not drawn to addictive substances or partying. We had a tame social life with a small number of both black and white friends, most of whom were his friends initially and therefore older than me. Steven was more like me in appearance than anyone I had yet known well, and I fit into a not-white and not-black niche for him. We were both Other-in-Self and Self-in-Other for one another. Much later, in his mid-thirties, when we were no longer a couple, he found a lifelong partner in a white woman. Steven was warm like my father, but he did not evaporate like my mother, and I felt safe and comfortable with him. I loved him deeply for a long time. He was the symbiotic partner that I had longed for since my infancy, and my early years with him were a new and wonderful phase of my life.

III

MOVING ON...
THE WHITE WORLD

From high school, I went to Bryn Mawr College near Philadelphia, Pennsylvania. Bryn Mawr is a small liberal arts college for women, one of the elite Seven Sisters colleges that existed at that time in tandem with the seven traditionally all-male Ivy League colleges. I was offered a full scholarship at the University of Pennsylvania in Philadelphia, which had just begun to admit women, but the large urban campus with high-rise dorms was daunting to me. Bryn Mawr was a small, pretty campus with Gothic architecture and a student body of mostly affluent and wealthy white women, most of whom had been privately educated. The campus atmosphere was highly intellectual and academically serious. I was able to make friends quickly and felt some sense of belonging, even though the class differences between my home town and others' social backgrounds often were stark. Apart from being wealthier, most of the other students also were better-educated than me and had better academic habits. Unlike my high school, which was not rigorous and in which I ranked eleventh in a class of over six hundred while rarely studying (spending lots of time with Steven), their high school educations were richer, broader, and offered better preparation for a serious college curriculum.

My first college year was tricky, as I had to adapt socially and scholastically. I had to find common ground with young women from mostly affluent to very wealthy backgrounds who had an array of experiences that I did not.

They were much more worldly than me. I had to study for the first time, and I did not really know how, and I had to battle my inner sense of not quite being up to par…I wasn't, and I had to catch up. I was separated from Steven for the first time and immersed in a community of mostly white people. I do not recall any black professors, although there might have been one or two somewhere. With the exception of one Spanish professor, all of the people who taught me were white.

Nonetheless, I came through the year well with good friends and decent grades. By the end of my second year, I was a strong student, if not in the top tier, and I graduated in three years with a 3.7 GPA and a Psychology major. I had become more independent and recognized my intellectual assets. I saw Steven every other weekend, sometimes in New Jersey and sometimes at Bryn Mawr, we exchanged letters, and we spoke every few days by phone. For much of each summer we lived together. It was not the pattern of daily contact that was in place during my high school years, but our relationship continued to develop.

For my college years, I had a regular babysitting job with a very wealthy and young Main Line family from "old money." The mother in the family had a well-known maiden name, and the father's surname was on the facades of buildings and streets in Philadelphia. Through that connection, I witnessed how families with long histories of inherited wealth lived. I learned some of their social rules and habits and saw the covert mechanisms by which they excluded others. I read the Social Register in the home library of their house, a compilation of profiles on the wealthiest, most socially desirable, and most influential families in the country. I was surprised at the rigid pettiness of many of the regulations and admittance criteria for inclusion in the Register. For starters, no blacks or Jews, and no one who had been divorced. Specific rules may have relaxed over time, but I doubt that the rigidity of the boundaries between those deemed "acceptable" and "unacceptable" has.

This family lived in a closed, private community of large brick or stone homes on large landscaped property lots. Many had in-ground swimming pools, which was unusual at the time. The community, a predecessor of gated communities, had a locked gate at the entrance. When new potential neighbors were looking for a home, the real estate company would mail out cards asking for comments on their suitability for the community from the residents. One was encouraged to disclose any pertinent information, including gossip. The mother in this family once told me that it is not money that ultimately counts in their social set but family lineage. Money is necessary but insufficient. For example, a very wealthy celebrity would not be eligible for the Social Register unless he or she also was from a proper family background.

The members of this social class are masterful at closing ranks for the purpose of creating Others. When the "nouveau riche" follow the "old money" to vacation places or residential areas or schools, the established wealthy just change course and find another more private enclave. They have a club that one cannot enter by choice or by money, no matter how accomplished, well-liked or well-regarded one is, and they ensure their privileged status with an iron grip on the power of exclusion. The epitome of Othering. My experience with this household was another education in itself.

At Bryn Mawr, I found a safe, non-threatening environment in which I was liked and successful. It was not perfect and, in hindsight, Penn might have been a better long-term choice, but I was educated well and fairly comfortable there…except for the specter of race that followed me. Early in my freshman year, I was approached by the small Black Student Organization to live in the Black Student House instead of the regular dorm. When I declined, I was shunned and had only the most casual of connection with any black student after that. The refrain played again: "Are you black or are you white?" However, the racial tone of my college was subdued and easier to manage than that of my high school.

Black students at Bryn Mawr segregated themselves in housing and social interactions; I only remember one black student who lived in my dorm. However, to my relief, there were no gross displays of animosity from blacks or whites. Everyone seemed friendly enough, if disconnected. With the exception of a few black students and a few international students in a few of my classes, none of whom became good friends of mine, I was in a virtually white world for the first time in my life. Only one white student ever questioned me about my racial or ethnic background, and she did so with curiosity, not hostility. She casually asked me one day simply: "What was it like having a black and a white parent?" No hostile confrontation, no racial test to pass, no threat. I found that I could answer her briefly, but equally casually, that it was "difficult."

After my college graduation, I went directly to graduate school. Being only twenty when I graduated, I was intimidated by the prospect of a serious job, so I did what I knew best…school. I decided to apply to Clinical Psychology graduate school because my favorite class was Abnormal Psychology, and I liked my field experience of working in a church school for autistic children. The mindset of a twenty-year-old…who felt a bit abnormal! Unconsciously, I needed a forum through which to explore the troubling pieces of my life and myself. I spent one year in a Master's program in Clinical Psychology attached to a hospital in Philadelphia and did well. There I had my first, albeit brief, experience of psychotherapy.

The following summer, I was accepted without a full admissions process into a psychoanalytic clinical psychology doctoral program that had lost an expected student and needed to fill a slot. I had a good academic and GRE record, and some graduate school success. I could apply and interview on short notice, I did not need financial aid, and I think because I would suffice as a minority, I was accepted almost immediately for the coming fall. By luck, happenstance, and the Power of the Unconscious, I had found my calling…or maybe my calling had found me!

At that time, Adelphi University on Long Island had one of the top clinical psychology Ph.D. programs in the country, and was one among only a few with a psychoanalytic orientation and a faculty predominantly composed of practicing psychoanalysts. The Institute, as it was known informally, was the flagship program of the university. Dr. Gordon Derner, then the founder and head of the Adelphi Clinical Psychology Doctoral Program, was very invested in diversity and had a specific quota of minority students for each entering class. Each class had five minority students, mostly black, out of twenty-five students, but the blacks did not self-segregate to the extent that they did at Bryn Mawr. As far as I remember, the black and white students in my class got along well and socialized a little, despite their varied backgrounds.

The black students were generally from poor or working-class families, and many of the white students were from affluent or wealthy homes, but the differences were masked by our common psychoanalytic interest. Yet, among all the Ph.D. classes, there were a few black students who felt it necessary to strike the hackneyed note: "Are you black or white?" That was accompanied by the usual blackness test. One man approached me about my lack of participation in the black student organization and in the Statistics study group that it was offering. He confronted me provocatively in the hallway around other students, evoking that same dread and fear that I carried with me as a child. The truth was that I had no intention of joining a black group, or any other group, and I was doing fine in Statistics.

To make an effort to get along, I did attend one Statistics study group meeting. However, I realized quickly that my math skills, while not great, were far above those of the others there. I did not want to be a "tutor" as I had been in elementary and junior high school by virtue of being a top student. So, I never returned. The black students stopped challenging me, but many were cold and unapproachable. Also, that same year I ended a burgeoning friendship with a Jewish girl when she began talking about "the schwartzes," and I made a lasting friendship with a black neighbor in my apartment building. I spent my graduate school years largely among other white students, made a few lifelong white friends, and had congenial acquaintances among just a handful of black students. It was, for the most part, comfortable enough interpersonally, but I still struggled within myself about race.

The study of psychoanalysis opened a newfound world of ideas and perspectives. The psychoanalytic education that I received at Adelphi was excellent, and my mind and personality were stimulated in novel and transformative ways. Yet, the study of psychoanalysis reinforced my white identifications. Once called "the Jewish science," perhaps an anachronistic phrase, psychoanalysis has been historically a largely white and upper-class endeavor. It requires intellectual and educational capabilities that not all whites or blacks have at their disposal, and it flourishes best in a sophisticated, intellectual milieu. It is generally possible as a clinical process only for people with time, introspective capacities, and financial resources. Developed among the white populations of Europe, for mostly Europeans, it has been divorced, in theory and practice, from the lifestyles of many blacks and poor whites in this country. As my father remarked when I was in graduate school: "Who can think about their dreams when they do not have shelter or enough food to eat?"

The percentage of black psychoanalysts in the 1970s was miniscule. Black clinical psychology students often were expected in sometimes understated ways to enter professional arenas related to urban black populations and their social and cultural challenges. This was the antithesis to the selective world of private therapy practice for which psychoanalytic training provided excellent preparation. Repeatedly, I found myself thinking, *Why should I (or any black person) automatically be relegated to working in a clinic for a low-moderate salary or treat patients on a low-fee basis when the white students were simply assumed to see full-fee patients and make much more money in an upscale private setting?* Blacks were assumed and expected to "give back to their communities," but whites were not constrained by any such supposition. Not surprisingly, I had no interest in directing my professional energies toward the black, urban community to which I felt that I did not owe anything. Another blackness test failed. I followed my psychoanalytic passion into the completion of psychoanalytic training and quickly moved into the "elite" world of private practice, never looking back.

Psychoanalysis in the 1970s in New York City was vibrant and opened new and exciting dimensions of understanding, heretofore never realized. My mind filled with new perspectives about myself, others, and the world. I was a superior clinical psychology student and developed a new sense of myself. It was the first time in my life that I enjoyed a sense of belonging and appreciation for my natural capacities and talents. I was interested in those around me, and I sought social connections openly. For the first time, I was mirrored in the Others near me, and they were mirrored in me. We were fans of psychoanalysis together!

I left graduate school with a number of good friends, male and female, with whom I have had varying degrees of contact over the years. Even in recent months, I have visited with a male and a female friend from graduate school who live many states away. My very close and dear friend, Cathy, is one of the lasting friends with whom I have frequent contact. She is extremely perceptive, loving, loyal, and highly creative. We came from and lived in very different surroundings but somehow resonated with each other in graduate school. Cathy is Jewish, from an affluent, highly-educated family and has a British mother. At the time we met, she was married to a medical student who grew up in the Hasidic community of Brooklyn.

Cathy is still the wife of the medical student-turned-cardiologist. She now also is the mother of four highly successful grown children, and an active member of her suburban religious community. She has worked professionally during much of her life, but her career has been subordinate to her husband. She has lived in the context of loving support and stability in a conventional and socially-sanctioned way. Our life structures have been very different, and we have struggled with very different things. I have envied her security and protection but came to learn over time that she has not always felt it as I see it. A tangled lesson in Self and Other, subjectivity and objectivity, which I cannot quite articulate, lies in that discrepancy.

Over our forty-seven-year friendship, the Otherness between us has faded as we have internalized each other. I have become Cathy's "corrective emotional experience," as she describes it, and she has become my "moreh" (Hebrew word for teacher). Before meeting Cathy, I had no exposure to religious or Orthodox Judaism and was unaware of the subtle cultural layers among Jews. Our connection added a new dimension to my array of identifications, piecemeal as they are. My familiarity with religious Judaism and Jewish people through her has allowed me to feel a tie to many people from whom I otherwise would have felt distant. They, like Cathy, are not fully Others now; they are some part of my Self.

IV

THE COMPLEXION OF MY INNER WORLD

My entrée into personal psychoanalysis opened a door to my inner world, a world new to me with both good and bad effects. I entered my own psychoanalysis in my first doctoral year, as did many of my academic peers. This was partly a requirement for school, partly a personal choice of each student, and partly a response to the easy reduced-fee arrangement between the Adelphi Clinical Psychology program and its affiliated Postdoctoral Psychoanalytic Training Program. At that time, most of the students, like me, entered formal psychoanalysis that required a minimum of three sessions per week, and others elected a less intense weekly or biweekly psychoanalytic therapy. At least one of us was an "old hat" at psychoanalysis, having had daily psychoanalysis for a few years before entering graduate school. Regardless of our therapy preferences, we all became engrossed in the study of psychoanalytic theory and practice and in our own therapy or analyses.

The ethnic, cultural, socioeconomic differences among us were overridden by our burgeoning knowledge and affinity for psychoanalysis in all its forms. We were all Others to each other in many ways, but in our psychoanalytic lives we reflected the Selves of one another. Although some of us were intellectually different from others in our theoretical interests, the umbrella of psychoanalysis united us with little rancor. The Freudians, the Ego Psychologists, the Kleinians, the Object-Relationists were like the animals on Bean Farm in my

Freddy the Pig books from childhood—we were chickens, ducks, pigs, cows, but we were all enjoying the same barnyard.

In the midst of this intellectual awakening, a dark cloud—and there always is one—also presented itself, the loss of my relationship with Steven. Our relationship ended rather abruptly for reasons peripheral to race, class, Self or Other, although we have sustained contact over the subsequent decades. At that time Steven's absence ushered in a long period of deep depression for me. My analyst at the time seemed to assume that the pain of this break-up was an episode, a liminal time that would pass, that I would heal, make new relationships, and move onto another more permanent bond. A typical course of events in which I tried to believe. After all, I was pretty, unusually smart, warm, likable, accomplished…why not?

Yet, the loss of this relationship proved to be a lasting trauma in my life…a devastating repetition of a wonderful connection that disappears and leaves me bereft and humiliated. It gave new meaning and weight to my early experience of having intimacy with my mother and losing it again and again. It disorganized me and left me acutely clinically depressed for well more than a year. I felt as though I had been ripped away from Steven with my skin left behind. Living in the rawness of this loss spanned my graduate school years and early twenties and reverberated into my forties. No one else ever broke my heart. Now, with the wisdom of maturity and hindsight, my understandings and feelings about Steven and our relationship are very different than they were at twenty-four, but I did not truly "get over" my relationship with Steven until middle-age. And I still grieve, not Steven as a person, but the loss of this piece of my life. Like Nanny, Steven had protected me from danger and compensated for the gaps in my frangible connection with my mother. Without him I was suddenly on my own, and the world was scary.

I spent a good bit of my first year in analysis talking about school, Steven, my parents, and race. Soon thereafter, the absence of Steven and all it raised filled my sessions. I lived simultaneously along two paths: an increasingly strong and secure one of intellectual and academic achievements with an upward trajectory that people around me recognized, and a second, hidden path of intimate relationships upon which I could barely stay above water. The ending of "Steven and Naomi" exposed a desolation that I was not able fully to overcome.

Along the upward path, I become more confident and accomplished, and developed strong professional skills. I did not reach any full resolution of racial matters, but I became more comfortable and more aligned with my white, affluent identifications, which led to less internal conflict. I no longer played the piano, but I began to ride horses (English style) frequently and seriously, another reflection of white affiliation. Yet, along the path of making an intimate relationship, I stumbled, had trouble getting up, feared I would drown, wanted to drown, and never did learn to swim.

I received my Ph.D. in Clinical Psychology at twenty-five years old after writing a dissertation on imaginary companions, and completing an internship at the same VA Hospital, ironically, where my father had been a patient after his war injury. I then completed a coveted Post-Doctoral Fellowship at an upscale private psychiatric clinic associated with a major New York City hospital. At graduation, I had a publication under my belt and an excellent job waiting for me as an Assistant Professor at a small Catholic university in New York City. There I taught undergraduate and graduate courses in the Psychology and Clinical Psychology programs, and soon thereafter opened a private practice in Manhattan. Years later, Karen Lombardi, by that time a good friend, covered my classes while I was on maternity leave. This university was again largely a white world, but I fit in smoothly…except for the refrain of, "Are you black or are you white?" Confronted that I should join the black faculty organization, I declined, a decision that marked me as "Other" and made me, again, a target for hostility.

One day I entered the faculty cafeteria with a white male friend of mine, another psychologist from the Psychology department. There were probably eight or ten black faculty seated at a long table, none of whom I knew. There were no whites at this table, and there were no blacks at other tables. This seemed to be the "black lunch table." As we walked past this table, one man confronted me loudly about why I was not sitting with them. The same old tune, just like public school, but from a grown, professional adult. This time, though, after a few years of psychoanalysis, and with professional confidence, I was able to respond without flinching or internally squirming: "I'm sitting with my friend and I do not know any of you," and then walked away.

Alongside my professional involvements with teaching and my private practice, I entered the Adelphi Postdoctoral Psychoanalytic Training program in order to officially become a psychoanalyst. There I met Karen Lombardi, and the seeds of our lasting intellectual/professional affiliation and personal friendship were sown. My affinity for psychoanalysis deepened. Those years of being a graduate and postdoctoral student, and moving into the professional world in New York City, were intellectually invigorating and brought many successes. Issues of race and class were at rest. Yet, my twenties continued to be colored with emotional pain and the resurgence of trauma, particularly the convergence of past and present despair and hopelessness.

Even though a depressive tone had permeated my childhood, there were also loving family connections, laughter, friends, and school successes, to balance the notes of sadness. I did not suffer poverty, abuse, or other social ills, and my parents had the education, awareness, and sophistication to provide desirable educational and personal experiences for me. My years with Steven were exciting and gratifying, and offered security, love, and affirmation in my developing femininity, even though some hard challenges crossed our path. All the positives of my younger years have mattered to me over the course of my life, but when my relationship with Steven ended, I landed in an interpersonal and emotional void. Another intimate relationship had abruptly evaporated, an echo of my attachment to my mother.

I remember having the momentary thought on our last day together that I would never meet anyone again after Steven…that this part of my life was over…and I panicked and became hysterical. This was the first of a few random, intrusive, disconnected thoughts at different points in my life that proved to be true. The Unconscious knows all! With a despair that had been mostly dormant for most of my life, I collapsed into a serious depression that lasted as an acute episode for most of two years and has continued as milder depressive pulls for the remainder of my life. The impact of my early childhood loss/ absence/ rejection colliding with my new jarring reality was crushing and horrible.

Through this acute depressive period, I excelled in graduate school, developed close friendships, and for the most part concealed my distress à la my childhood coping style. The clinical term "smiling depression" was apt. However, despite being in analysis four times weekly, I remained crippled in other ways. Having been only with Steven since the age of fourteen, I did not know how to deal with dating at all; I hated it. I felt totally out-of-place around men, not feeling at ease with someone who was not familiar and who did not already know me intimately. Despite the attempts that I could and did make, albeit not frequently, I never met anyone romantically special, ever, in the daily course of my life. I was psychologically incapable of navigating the singles life in New York City in the late 1970s and early 1980s. Although I was quite pretty, well-liked and personable, and very well-dressed, I felt vulnerable and exposed. I quickly retreated from any social arenas that seemed at all perilous, and I suffered inwardly with sharp feelings of shame, inadequacy, and a deep sense of being "defective." I think that I would have made a really good identical twin, but I was terrible at being single.

In my early thirties, I tried again to form a serious relationship with a man. I was not in love with this man, but he was a very reasonable choice of partner for me, we had many similarities, and I was quite fond of him. When that effort failed, I gave up trying. I did not completely relinquish hope right then, but I stopped putting effort into searching for an intimate partner. I was moving toward being "done," but it would take another decade of unresponsiveness from the Universe before enough disappointment was enough. This man and I have remained close friends. Thirty years later, he expressed sincere and deep regrets and apologies that he foreclosed our earlier relationship, but by then he was married. He broached the idea of divorcing his wife to reconnect with me, but we lived on opposite coasts, I was not open to that arrangement, and thirty years had passed. In many ways, we were well-matched even then, but too little, too late. Quite sad.

In reaction to the shame and defective feelings that permeated my twenties, I became rather perfectionistic about my clothing, buying mostly beautiful, expensive clothing as was so easy in Manhattan in those years. In retrospect, I understood this as a recapitulation of my early childhood ventures with my mother, who, in her love for New York City and for me, would take me to upscale Manhattan department stores and buy me pricey, unusual outfits. At six, my mother bought me an expensive turquoise dress with a small leafy black pattern from Lord and Taylor that I especially wanted. (In the cover photo of this book, I am wearing this dress.) Twenty years later, Lord and Taylor was my favorite department store. These shopping expeditions expressed race and class codes that as a child kept me separate from my peers but strengthened the bond between my mother and me. In turn, in my young adult years, lovely clothing unconsciously symbolized protection by my mother, bolstered my sense of wholeness, and provided comfort when I felt fractured.

Dressing with panache as a young woman also brought admiration from my peers and reinforced my white, upper middle-class identifications that were representations of my mother. I could fit into almost anything in a small size, and I developed a flair for color and style. However, I was overly sensitive about any flaws in my clothes or mismatched accessories. I had similar psychophysical reactions to clothing flaws as I did to scratchy fabrics as a young girl, and I could become obsessed and compulsive about avoiding them. I generally preferred only soft fabrics and looser styles and was quite discomfited by any stain or tear that I missed while dressing. In contrast to my inner experience of myself, a good friend once told me that my perfectionistic appearance and seeming confidence made me seem unapproachable to her. Luckily, I approached her and we became close friends for years.

Unconsciously, flaws and accessory mishaps meant exposure of my defects, shame, and disunity in my Self, but when all was in place I felt pretty and feminine in a way that I could not otherwise. Although later the mess and expense of babies and young children, especially baby vomit on a silk blouse, pushed me to choose a more practical wardrobe, my affinity for lovely clothing still hangs at spots in my closet. And I still have some tension around things that are broken, damaged, blemished.

Despite my exterior, I often felt suffused with shame, sometimes suicidal, and unable to tolerate "being in my own skin." I sometimes had a sensation that my feelings were chopped off so that raw nerve endings stuck out into the world, perhaps reminiscent of the "abrasive womb." Wearing lovely, soft clothing soothed me physically and emotionally. At one point, I described my feeling about myself to my analyst as being "just a head and an expensive dress with no body underneath." I dreamt of walking into my dark apartment, tripping over something, and turning on a light, only to see body parts strewn across the floor. At another much later point, I dreamt of being in water up to my neck on a warm, sunny day. I looked around me and all was peaceful and pleasant. Then I looked down into the water and saw that the lower half of my body was shredded and bleeding.

At first after the breakup with Steven, the compliments and assurances of others buoyed me, but as the months and years alone went on, optimism dwindled and my feelings of failure, inadequacy, and shame mounted, until I could no longer hold out hope for finding a partner in the face of endless emptiness. The empty platitudes that were extended with good intentions, but proved to be untrue, such as "there's someone for everyone," "once you stop looking, you will meet someone," "just live your life and someone will find you," only inflamed my sense of inadequacy. I felt like I was slipping into an abyss while everyone else was on solid ground, together, having a good time, oblivious. I was alone and unable to comprehend a world that they negotiated easily. We were just Others with superficial connections that disguised my isolation and defectiveness.

In general, my friends came from two basic groups: young marrieds, or single, sexually casual women (pre-AIDS) who always had a man or men in their lives and in their beds. Either they did not need to look for a man or they had no trouble finding many. Neither reflected my experience, and I felt isolated from them around this. My married friends had met their husbands in college with little or no effort, a circumstance distressing to me because it seemed so unfair. (I had not yet comprehended that most of life is unfair to someone.) One of my friends who engaged easily in casual sex was perplexed about why I did not want to go to clubs with her and meet guys. Once I did go, and she left with a random man, leaving me to travel home by myself. I, of course, found no one interesting there and made no contact with anyone. I went home immobilized and heartsick, barely able not to sob on the subway, and I never tried that again.

As this was happening in my external life, inwardly my thoughts and emotions were changing. I wanted to marry and have a conventional family, but my wish for a child was steadily intensifying until it seemed to find a life of its own. The theme of babies arose in my analysis through repetitive dreams and associations, and in my life through a preoccupation with fantasies of motherhood increasingly disconnected from thoughts of marriage. I do believe that if I had met someone naturally, I could and would have formed an intimate relationship. I was not disabled regarding intimacy, but I could not expose myself, my yearnings, or my feelings without it. I could barely tolerate being aware of them myself because of the shame elicited by their very presence in the absence of a response from the world. Here, is the reflection of being unable to keep my mother's attention, the exposure of my inadequacy in doing so, and the crippling feeling of vulnerability and complete rejection. I had never internalized enough protectiveness, and I did not develop tough-enough skin to shield me until many decades later.

The most painful psychic element for me all my life is the exposure of unmet needs—feeling not just unloved, but unlovable, experiencing myself as the baby whose longings have been stimulated, but whose mother has evaporated. Toughness only developed in my early forties, after I relinquished Hope and closed my feelings down. The ordeals that forced me to change from being sweet, gentle, naively accommodating, and a bit dependent eventually fueled a steely cynicism that has safeguarded my vulnerabilities and helped me stay upright alone. Yet, in my mid-twenties, I was filled with loneliness and acute longings for intimacy, and I teetered on the edge of a deep sense of inadequacy and profound humiliation.

At the age of twenty-nine, some calming of my acute distress had begun to occur, although the wounds were still palpable. My professional life was swimming along smoothly, as it always had. Although I had not found my stride with men, I had dragged myself off the drowning path. I struggled with shame and feeling defective, but otherwise my head was above water. I had a small circle of good friends, I rode horses a few times weekly, which I loved and did into my fifties, and I was very pleased with my living space. I still found it very painful to watch my peers marry and have children, and I felt inadequate for not being able to do so, despite my professional achievements. A particular misery that I felt every day was the sense that my aloneness broadcast my inadequacy as a woman, that my innermost feelings were exposed and starkly evident through my life circumstance. Obviously this was not the case, but it felt true. With clothes, smiles, and social graces I disguised it all well. Yet, neither my analysis nor the Universe were truly healing my pain, so I decided it was time to heal myself.

I turned sharply in a new direction. I decided to have a child alone—figuratively, to get a jelly doughnut for myself. If the universe was not going to feed me a meal, I was going to stop asking for one…a jelly doughnut would do. I was confident that I could raise a child well financially and emotionally, and I KNEW intuitively that being a mother would ease my woe. At that time, single parenthood was not regarded positively and likely to be a lonely enterprise even in Manhattan. I attended a few meetings with maybe ten to fifteen people of a then new support organization in Manhattan that now is international called Single Mothers by Choice, but as an only child who does not like or join groups, I did not continue an association with them. (In a slip-of-the-tongue, I once referred to this group as "Single Mothers without Choice" —maybe more to the point.)

When a colleague entered early menopause childless at thirty-three, which unnerved me, I did not waste a moment. I changed trajectories then and there. Within a few months I was pregnant and within a year or so I was the mother of a baby son. I named him Philip, a name that means "lover of horses," only realizing in his infancy that it unconsciously meant to me "Fill up." HA! One can never fool one's Unconscious! With my son, I was now a Self with an Other. I had a new facet to my identity and an affirmation of my womanhood, which years alone had eroded. I was no longer just a head with an expensive dress; I now had a "filled-up" body.

Naively, I thought that having a child on my own would not preclude me from forming an intimate relationship in the future. A few years later, I learned differently. Research from the 1980s showed that women who deliberately had children alone without fathers involved (excluding divorced and widowed women, and women in intimate partnerships with men) almost never made subsequent lasting relationships, unlike divorced, widowed, partnered women who do. Their financial and emotional independence, which may have pre-dated their motherhood, and their willingness to forego living with a man, were too threatening to potential partners. The prospect of parenting a child who does not have a father to share the fatherly obligations portended too much paternal responsibility for many men. The research sample was small, the woman were older than me and, of course, this may be different now, thirty-five or forty years later, but a few of my own experiences at the time supported this dismaying conclusion.

Some have told me that I foreclosed on intimacy prematurely, that I was too young, that I could have waited even eight or ten years to see what might have happened. Perhaps so, but I could not continue on without some closeness in my life. I had reached the end of that road. Many who did wait developed infertility issues or pregnancy complications that sometimes, in those years particularly, were not remediable. This was a risk that I was not willing to take and psychologically could not endure. I simply would not have been able to live a life with neither a husband nor a child; a husband was desirable, but psychically a child was imperative. Due to my prenatal and early infancy experience with my mother, and the damage to my sense of womanhood in those years, I had a pressing need, a craving, to create, bear, and nurse my child that precluded any consideration of adoption or of a childless life.

Being released from longing and expectation by the acceptance of a certain void in my life, and a new direction, brought great relief. I was no longer tormented by empty Hope and Optimism. I no longer suffered with wanting someone only to have him evaporate or fail to appear, or with envy for those who created a dyad effortlessly, and my raw feelings were no longer exposed to the harshness of that reality. I was headed on a new journey that did not include those states of mind or soul. So, by thirty, a bit impulsively, I made a family in the form that was available to me. Unconsciously, however, I did repeat a pattern of my own family—unconventional and likely to be Other.

I turned out to be good at raising children alone. I was not overwhelmed by usual parenting demands, I was self-reliant and self-sufficient, I did not suffer with guilt that my children did not have a father, and I found it simple to be clear, honest, and straightforward with them about their life circumstance. Remarkably, pregnancy and motherhood "cured" me as psychoanalysis had not. Despite some lonely moments, and being out-of-step at times with other young families, I have no longer felt inadequate or defective. After holding my newborn babes in my arms, I felt whole. Sometimes impulsivity works!

During my young-to-middle-adult years, I exchanged independence for a counter-dependence that served me well. I have not considered myself to be a "Single Mother." Singlehood is my circumstance, but it has not been my identity. I am a mother, a psychoanalyst, a friend, a daughter, an author, and a few other mini-Selves. I stopped looking to an imagined or actual Other for companionship, support, security, identity, or to move my life forward. I became accountable and responsible only to myself. My rather distant and cool adult relationship with my mother warmed considerably as we shared a love for my offspring. I could bemoan the real burdens that come with an unattached life, but I also enjoyed its freedoms. When my son was a bit over one-year old, I moved from New York City to California to live in the sunshine, near the beach, without having to consult with anyone, and I spent twelve productive years there.

In the process of relinquishing the wish for an intimate bond, I bore and raised two children alone. (One jelly doughnut was not quite enough.) The years of active motherhood were both gratifying and stressful. They brought joy and connections with other mothers, but also periods of anxiety and depression, as can be the case for mothers in all family scenarios. After my second child, a girl, was born, I developed nightmares of men breaking into my house and hurting my children. A jumble of apprehensions about having the sole responsibility for two children that crept into my mind, pressing feelings of vulnerability occasioned by the French doors in my bedroom that led to the backyard, and the final letting-go of the idea of a relationship with a man, led me into a long second analysis. When my daughter was two months old, I took to hiding a baseball bat under my bed for protection, which prompted me to call an analyst. Within a month or two of starting my second analysis, these symptoms receded, and my life beyond this narrative took its first steps.

As my children entered middle childhood, the window for the conventional nuclear family life that I wanted had pretty much closed, and the remaining alternatives held little appeal for me. I did not wish to mother a man's existing children, I did not greatly desire a third child, and I did not long just for companionship even though loneliness sometimes lurked. Intimacy and the opportunity to build a life with someone that I did desire did not materialize and just did not seem to be in the cards. After years examining, blaming, berating myself for being alone without any clear sense of what I did wrong or what I should be doing, I finally understood that most of my situation was just bad luck. It was simply not something that I could control. Whatever my personal flaws and failings were, they were no worse and likely far less than those of many people with spouses or partners. With those realizations, I created safeguards around my vulnerabilities, and settled into the life that I had, but inwardly and outwardly withdrew. In my early forties, I just lost interest and emotion around intimacy; I was truly "done" with longing and searching, and so I have remained.

My parents were supportive and involved with my family of two young children. My mother cared for my son while I worked until we moved to Southern California. In the baby years, they gave me the financial means to stay at home for most of the first year of each infant's life, and then to hire a wonderful, loving nanny when Clara was born, a young college student named Elyse. I have often said that I won the nanny lottery! My father came to California at least twice to see us before his death. He traveled with my mother but endured a trip that was arduous given his age and disability. In turn, we visited my parents a few times before my father's death, and continued to visit back-and-forth with my mother until her early eighties when she became too old to travel from New Jersey to California by herself. Elyse was the nanny for my children for many years, she met my parents, and we met hers. She has remained in the family. All of us see her, talk to her, love her, and consider her one of us.

I have felt guilty that I "disappeared" on my parents, taking their only grandchild across the country. I was selfishly preoccupied…and oblivious. My mother expressed to me that my father was quite upset that I moved so far away, but I think both were pained by my action. Nonetheless, my mother explained to my father that I needed to live my life as I saw fit, and they did not burden me with their feelings. My mother was wise in this as she was in many things. Both of my parents were supportive and loving through their silent and hidden tears. On the days right before we left for California, my mother helped me pack our last things, put me and her baby grandson in a taxi headed to the airport, and waved us off. I imagine now, as a grandmother myself, that doing so was heart-wrenching for her.

My redemption has been the reality that if I had not moved to California, I would not have had my dear Clara. Another baby perhaps, but not my Clara. My parents, my analyst, and my close friends were supportive presences in the background, but the child-rearing experience was mine alone all the way through. With delight, I brought home two beautiful newborn babies, four years apart…by myself. Two decades later, with pride and pleasure, I celebrated their college graduations…by myself.

My years of psychoanalysis, which overlay much of my quotidian life, generated its own Self—my overly-analyzed Self. Since my analyses, nothing about my emotional Self exists apart from the imprints of my early experiences. Although my private pain has eased, receding from my immediate experience much of the time, it has become easily accessible and easily stimulated. Everything is felt in facets and layers, and it can be tiring to figure out which facet or layer fits which situation or relationship. My thoughts are free-flowing and abundant, but sometimes idiosyncratic to me and not understood by others. Sometimes, ancient emotions or associations peculiar to me pop into the forefront of my mind intrusively. Though I have conquered and integrated much of the strain from my childhood and early adulthood, the residue remains. Sometimes it is a shadow in the background just beyond easy reach, and sometimes a palpable, immediate presence, but I cannot deny or repress emotions or thoughts very well. I can never feel, or live, as if they have not been. I cannot return to "blissful ignorance." In many ways, it is more difficult to connect with and feel integrated around others.

Paradoxically, those of us who have been in lengthy psychoanalysis can become "too aware," hamstrung by our insight and less able to fit in with ordinary society. We hold expectations and desires for others' awareness and introspection that they cannot meet, and we seldom see things at face value as most other people do much of the time. We notice details and meanings in things to which others are oblivious, and we have capacities for understanding feelings and the impact of life events that are not easily reciprocated. We have a hyper-awareness of potentially troublesome dynamics in people around us that can keep us apart from others. We have a worldview that is not always in sync with those near us. We may have associative trains of thought that others cannot follow. We develop a Self that is not easily reflected in the Other, compounding loneliness, alienation, frustration, and disappointment.

The potentially transformational character of psychoanalysis does not always, or only, move one toward richer relationships with others, even though it may enrich one's inner relationship with himself or herself. Psychoanalysis can make one lonely. All things cannot be healed.

Such is my story.

V

WORDS TO THE WISE

I will pause here with a short legacy of insights garnered from my childhood, my early life, and my reflections upon them. These are incomplete thoughts, for you, the reader, to contemplate if you wish. I have only thoughts with few answers to the questions they may elicit.

1. A genie, once released from the bottle, cannot be contained again. Genies do not like to be contained, and if contained they will haunt you. A dilemma.
2. Everything that we experience from before birth on becomes Self. We cannot remove these experiences, destroy them, or escape them. We can only shift them around, add to them, and embrace them. Some things we absorb from the psyches of our parents and these elements originate as Other. Yet, once we experience them, they become Self. Eventually, we must find a way to embrace all psychic elements if we are to feel whole.
3. In any context, the Other is more a product of our minds than an external reality. This is useful to remember when you feel unfairly judged or emotionally attacked by someone—that person is reacting to something in him or herself, more than to something in you. Self-reflection may be important in such situations, but understanding the origins of the attack or judgments in the Other often is more

useful. However, the converse of this dynamic is true when you are the one reacting unfairly or disproportionately…then it is time to look inward.
4. Race and Class are psychic elements of Self that have been rejected and relegated to the realm of Other, not objective factors. We have separated them from us, but they are not truly separate.
5. Everything influences everything else, life cannot be unwound, all things have infinite causes, infinite effects, and infinite reverberations. There is no single cause and no single effect. Understanding anything always requires a recognition and appreciation of context and frame of reference.
6. We can only see part of the elephant. We may feel that we know or understand ourselves, or another, but the whole elephant will forever evade our grasp. Sometimes things appear clearly black or white, but much of Life is lived in the gray…or the beige.
7. Love and Hate, Good and Evil, rarely if ever, come in pure form. Disentangling them, and accepting their entanglement, are how we come to understand ourselves and others. But be forewarned—the road to insight has no natural end. There will always be more complexities to unravel and more contradictions to accept.
8. If we seek to sustain any relationship, we need to be more loving than hating—able to temper our inevitable hatred with the accessibility of love. Gaps between us can be tolerated and sometimes desirable, but chasms, abysses, gulfs are breeding grounds for isolation and despair—killing fields for love of self and others. If we are mindful and lucky, our relationships will fill with more love than hate.
9. Hope and Optimism are projections from one's psyche into one's fantasy of the future. They are not real, not external to us, and they have no substance other than what one assigns them. Possibility is infinite, but Hope and Optimism are fueled by our needs and sometimes must be abandoned in order to survive.
10. Psychoanalysts call "acting-out" what everyone else calls Life!

EPILOGUE

Over the decades following my young adulthood, I have become increasingly comfortable with relative solitude. I am not completely isolated, but socially I mostly prefer to be by myself, with my children, or on occasion with one of a few close friends. I do maintain phone contact with a good number of friends from earlier in my life. In relative aloneness, I have returned to my childhood self over the years, introverted and living in my mind. Nonetheless, anxiety about isolation creeps into my consciousness in long-standing fears of open, unbounded spaces, abysses, or voids. Occasionally from childhood on, I have found myself struggling with urges to throw myself off cliffs, I have come close to panic on the brink of snorkeling or water skiing (being in open water alone without a connection to a stable object), and I avoid heights because I am drawn to fantasies of jumping from them. These persistent themes are representations of the frightening emptiness between my mother and myself, which I simultaneously abhor and desire.

Although in moments I have longed to reach across these empty spaces and connect with the other side (symbolically my mother), and as an extension of this dynamic, to connect with others, but the chasm between us seems daunting and perilous. In the end, safety and solid ground win out, even if the price is isolation. As I write this, one particular memory of a void comes to mind. Nanny and I are walking by an empty elevator shaft in a Manhattan office building. The shaft has no door or barrier. I am curious and want to peer into the shaft. Nanny grasps my hand firmly, but I steal a quick glance before we pass by. The deep, dark, empty hole is shocking, alarming, but I want to keep looking at it. Once again, Nanny protects me, keeps me safe. But she is no longer here. The only security that I can access for myself is to stand far away from the edge, away from both temptation and danger, to isolate myself.

Being alone, ensconced in solitude, at times reclusive, has become my comfort zone. In comparison to most other people, I have much less need for social contact, partnership, social approval, or community. I do not identify with any group and, apart from a few decades-old friendships, relationships with my children and in my work, and finding occasional satisfaction in one-on-one socialization, I keep away from people. After many years of teaching and sharing a professional office environment with one other person, I now practice solo and am very happy to be doing so. The desire for closeness and energy for socialization that was alive in my early adulthood has been burned away by disappointment, frustration, and time. Closeness no longer seems as reassuring, and most ordinary social contacts feel empty and undesirable. I have learned to live with a good bit of emotional deprivation and to avoid too much vulnerability. I no longer want the experiences that I once yearned for, and it is now a comfort to be mostly alone and keep my own company.

I also have made peace with my dysthymic nature. Having tried a few antidepressants at different points over the decades, all of which helped temporarily until they didn't, I stopped seeking relief from myself. Life changes, circumstances shift, moods fluctuate, but my emotional set-point always has had a dispirited cast. So be it. When I look around me at the world, its history, and its people, the drama mask of Tragedy, not the mask of Comedy, seems to have the upper hand in the human condition. As the British psychologist Richard Bentall, who has a background in Philosophy, proposed in 1992, perhaps happiness, "a statistical abnormality" with "debilitating consequences," (the effects of denial) should be classified as a psychiatric disorder. As Southerners sometimes say: I "might-could" go along with that!

The lasting fallout from the more harrowing aspects of my life is not so much constant depression as a loss of Hope or Optimism. I can express hopefulness about minor and generic things, such as the weather or if the train will come in time or "I hope she will come for dinner," but in the larger realms of living I do not traffic in Hope. I am now a firm realist with a cynical, blunt edge and little place for optimism or hopefulness. Things are as they are, not as they might be, should be, could be. I have suffered too much disappointment to live in a realm of desire and wish. The risk of dark possibilities is always active for me. I do not "sing in the rain."

I do, though, have a capacity to experience happiness, I often am quite compassionate and generous, and I have a good, albeit sarcastic, sense of humor. These characteristics combine identifications with both of my parents. With the exception of those who specialize in denial and idealism, people tend to find me warm and easy to be with, at least superficially, although I have a definite dark side that they may not see. I have a good bit of my mother's gentleness and my father's warmth, but I harbor anger and depression that surface intermittently, and I can be harshly honest. I do not have patience with people who lean toward denial, idealization, or excessive positivity. I respond to them with edgy irritability and react inwardly with depression. In fact, I am not a very patient person. In my younger years, I was fast-paced—thinking, speaking, walking quickly. I am slower now in those ways but still tend to be impatient about things and easily frustrated with people who live by a slower tempo.

Through the unconscious identifications with and the conscious values expressed by my parents, I began my adult life with idealism and humanitarian ideas and sensitivities. I have kept some of their humanistic sensibility, but not their idealism. As you now know, my mother was an unwavering idealist always, and my father held onto his humanistic beliefs through trauma, pain, sharp disappointments, alcoholism, depression. I could not do so. Unlike for them, the depth of the sensibilities that my parents showed me did not survive the onslaught of the vicissitudes of living that I encountered along my way. As my hurt and frustration accumulated, bitterness and a diminished attraction to people infiltrated the naive openness that I enjoyed into my twenties. I am not enamored with the human species. Dogs and horses, and probably bonobos, are better.

At moments of acute misanthropy, I find myself giving up on humanity and defaulting to the conclusion that we, humans, are just a bad species—violent, greedy, clannish, destructive, like our close chimpanzee cousins. At times, I can wish not to be a human being, but, alas, that is not changeable. Some better individuals are interspersed among us humans, but as a whole we have little capacity for redemption. The human brain has become an over-evolved organ, wreaking havoc on itself and others, and possibly fated to be the instrument of our collective demise. Most of the good we do is reparation for what we have destroyed, and then we go on to destroy similarly again.

My preference for solitude sometimes is lonely, but it is always gentler and safer than being too exposed to the social world. At this point in my life, I would not choose to relinquish it. I have learned to manage my moods fairly well, but also to create room in my mental life and in my lifestyle for some depression and not to run from it. It will pass, come again, pass again, return…Yet, with a nod to the early memories with which I began this memoir, I can get jelly doughnuts for myself, I do not need my father to catch me, and, having exchanged my white leather baby shoes for adult shoes, I can walk along my own path.

Nevertheless, perhaps I have written this autobiographical narrative in my older years to retrace my steps. I had a dream while finishing this book about finally engaging with the toddler from my childhood dream life and integrating all that she/he encapsulated. In my recent dream, the toddler, a girl now, is no longer wearing blue overalls, but has on an outfit designed for a young girl. Perhaps she is no longer "blue overall," but in the moment of the dream she collapses on the floor, sobbing hysterically as I am trying to leave her. I think with angry annoyance: *Where is her mother? Her mother is responsible for her, not me!* Yet, this time in my dream, while recognizing my anger, I turn back and embrace her; I tend to her instead of wanting her to tend to me. Despite not appearing in any of my dreams for over forty years, the toddler remained…waiting. As do our traumas and emotions.

On a lighter note: My affinity for one-on-one relationships and for the solitude that protected me as a child were two threads that also led me to the practice of psychoanalysis. I answered my calling and professionally never looked back. Completing psychoanalytic training and becoming a psychoanalyst proved to be an excellent fit for me. I have continued to work as a clinical psychologist and analyst in private practice and academia in New York City, Southern California, and Georgia, writing professional papers and books and becoming a Supervising and Training Analyst for two institutes during my California days. I raised two successful, competent, and very decent children of whom I am most proud. They are grown adults now with their own race and class, Self and Other dynamics and idiosyncrasies, but they seem to be swimming along more smoothly than I did. I have solid loving bonds with both of my children, although each relationship has its warts, as does their relationship with each other.

My father died of cancer, probably related to his war wound, at the same VA hospital where he refused alcoholism treatment. He was almost eighty. My father had returned from war with newfound disillusionment and anguish to a loving wife who carried the light of hope and optimism in her heart.

Ultimately, over the years, my mother's lighter mood did not prevail against my father's adversity and growing despair. Although he continued with determination to confront injustice, his energy waned as the years passed. The accumulation of his life traumas and the futility of his efforts for social and political change instilled a growing depression that eventually enveloped him.

A troubled soul most of his life, my father was dejected and cantankerous in his last years, but he never relinquished his humanitarian principles or his capacities for love and commitment. He died having shared in the first years of his grandchildren's lives, taking delight in them. In the last year of his life, my active, fractious three-year-old daughter spent an entire afternoon sitting quietly beside her grandfather on my parent's couch, just chattering away. They were engrossed in one another. My father, who adored her spirit, admitted that he could not understand much of what she said, but in his words: "My heart knew what she meant." I know that he felt secure in my love and respect for him and in the unyielding love and understanding of my mother, despite being irascible about most other things. My mother recounted that in one of the last days of my father's life when he was slipping in and out of consciousness in his hospital bed, he awoke, reached for her hand, and said: "You and me against the world."

My mother died turning ninety-four. She remained in sound mind until her very last days and in good health until her heart failed in the last years of her life. My son made it a "mitzvah" to visit her in New Jersey once or twice every semester while he was in college at Yale. She had taken care of him as a baby, and he saw that she was cared for well in those years. My daughter, who lived in France during the last few years of my mother's life, came to see her grandmother directly from Kennedy Airport every time she visited home. My mother and I did not live near each other after I moved to California, but I was in close phone contact with her and, as I mentioned, visited her once or twice a year after she could no longer travel to the West Coast. As her health weakened in the last years of her life, my mother had a caring and attentive aide who was with her daily. I visited her a month before her death. I believe that my mother generally felt safe, loved, and securely "held."

My mother was a believer in Good, although not in God, all the way through. Perhaps this attitude was partly a residual thread of the Catholic upbringing that she eschewed as an adult, and perhaps it reflected her mother's fervent belief that "everyone has a soul." Unlike my father and me, who tried to accept and balance the Good, the Bad, and the Ugly, my mother sincerely believed that eventually human Goodness would prevail. She addressed herself to the better side of everyone, often to my great annoyance. Her difficulty being angry, cynical, or irreverent counter-balanced my father's temperament, but kept her from having a good sense of humor. There is no humor without access to anger - anger and irreverence are what make 'funny' funny and what make people laugh. Unlike my father who could be quite angry and very funny, my mother was gentle, kind, fair, and Good until the end, but rarely humorous.

My mother reminded me of the Swiss, who also do not seem to have a good sense of humor.

Life in Switzerland seems too easy, too secure, and too comfortable for people to be angry enough for good humor, or at least not consistently angry enough for anger to permeate the culture. Without anger, attempts at humor are infantile and fall flat. In recent years, I have heard Swiss men laugh heartily at old jokes from the 1940s, but perceive only the hostility in irreverence without comprehending the humor in the sarcasm. I have only one friend who is like my mother, consistently good, kind, and gentle in word and action. Usually, people who are idealistic and seldom angry draw out my cynicism and annoy or anger me, but I have known this friend for thirty years, and I forgive her this fault. I do appreciate her and am very fond of her, but luckily for me and my mood she lives far away.

Until two days before her death, my mother had been hospitalized only twice…to give birth to me, and in her eighties when she fell and fractured her pelvis on the way back from voting for Obama. She said that she fell because she was distracted by her excitement about his possible election and tripped. At eighty-six after returning from a theater performance, my mother walked up eleven flights of stairs to her apartment one night alone, using a stairwell when the building's elevator broke down. In recounting this to me and in response to my surprise, she stated, in her typically modest manner: "But, dear, I stopped and rested every three or four flights." HA! I am relieved that she did not have a physical collapse alone in that stairwell, and I am also relieved that neither she, nor my father, lived to see what has transpired in this country after Obama's presidency.

A few years after my father died, my mother moved from my childhood home to senior housing, where she lived independently until her death. She made friends with other black and white residents, most of whom were uneducated and probably far less intellectual than her, but she had the ability to overlook such details and engage with their other attributes. At the end, her years of living in a largely black community seemed to pay off well. Frail, small, at ninety lbs., and over ninety years old with a fanny pack around her waist and a cane in her hand, my mother walked to the grocery store, doctors' offices, in the park near her apartment building, and got on buses by herself in a deteriorating and not always safe neighborhood without ever being accosted. She had a friendly greeting for everyone, even those who looked homeless or intoxicated, never expressing, and perhaps never feeling, disdain or fear. She involved herself for quite a few years teaching reading literacy to adults who were unable to read or write, easily appreciating them for their personal qualities, not just valuing their intelligence, education, or accomplishments (as I am prone to do). People knew her in the neighborhood and, I believe, gave her space and protection to be herself, as she did with them.

My mother's love for New York City continued into her last years. Through her eighties, she traveled alone on trains and buses into "the City" to attend ballet and music performances, meet a close friend, and join a protest march against the Iraq War. She felt a bit intimidated by the size of the crowd at this march, given her age and frailty, so she attached herself to a group of black church women who guarded her from the pushing crowd. Totally my mother!! As she became elderly, especially after my father's death, my mother appeared more and more like a black woman of very light complexion…more and more like my aunt, Noni. Unconsciously, she internalized my father and "became" him, a transformation from Self and Other to Self-in-Other. Amidst the black church women, except for her atheism, my mom fit right in!

Over the course of my adulthood and after years of psychoanalysis, my hurt and angry feelings about my parents subsided. We had loving and consistent relatedness, if not emotional closeness. After years of reflection, I no longer needed my mother or father to understand me, because I understood them. It would be nice to conclude that all my racial issues resolved in the end. But that would be disingenuous. There is no resolution for me, or for this country at this time, in the area of race. Perhaps the younger generation of biracial individuals will have better experiences. For me, there has been just the same resounding question: are you black or white?

Over the years, I semi-consciously made a choice. I live in an affluent white world because it is just simpler and more comfortable. As Isabel Wilkerson might discuss it, I landed within the dominant caste in American society. I am not among the wealthiest affluent classes, but I hold my own among the educated upper-middle class and dip my toes in richer waters from time-to-time. I do frequently find myself betwixt and between opposing factions in many aspects of living, including race, class, and everyday situations. Not quite this and not quite that. I rarely have conscious intent to seek out this position, but there I am over and over again. Not quite this and not quite that.

There has been no option for me to live in black and white worlds equally. Black culture, like white culture, is not monolithic, but in my life it has been more treacherous. The white world has been more welcoming. I have some understanding of and sensitivity to many facets of black culture, but I do not much feel a part of it. It is more Other than Self. I also do not identify as "biracial" because I do not know what that means in reference to a cultural or ethnic identity. It may be genetically relevant, but it has no meaning for me as a cultural affiliation; I do not see a definable "biracial" culture with which to identify…or dis-identify. Black people sometimes recognize my mixed heritage, but white people almost never do, despite subliminally perceiving something unusual in my features. In recent years, the question, "Are you black or are you white?" has morphed into a more subtle: "What is your nationality/ethnic background/heritage?" But the subtext is the same: "Are you black or are you white?" My answer to the question now is: "Neither."

In early 2019, I was present at the birth of my beautiful grandson, Lee, my daughter's child. He is half-Japanese, a new contribution to our family and to our family gene pool. Lee is Other but with aspects of Self that I experience as affirming. His skin tone is more like mine than that of either of my children. He has dark, almond-shaped eyes that reflect his Japanese genes, combined with his mother's round nose and cheeks that scream, "Rucker!" He is affectionate, smart, handsome, and thriving, presenting all the wonders of healthy development. And best of all, in contrast to the sadness I expressed at age two, he spontaneously said to me at that same age, "I'm happy, Nana! Are you happy?" My answer was: I'm happy because I'm with you."

He is adored.

My daughter is a geologist-geophysicist with a global engineering and design firm and an outstanding mother—consistently, close, loving, and understanding of Lee's individual personality and needs. Her spouse offers their son love and consistency every day. My son is an internationally recognized newspaper journalist and editor who makes time in a relentless schedule to be a loving uncle. He is pleased to do so, and his growing bond with his nephew reflects this. Lee is a delight and has brought joy to all our lives. I do worry for the sociocultural issues he may face beyond the cocoon of his parents and close family. Lee lives within an unconventional family in a very conservative community with very few, if any, Asian members. My heart breaks if I think too deeply about this situation. I remind myself that his circumstances are not identical to mine, nor is his nature. The coloring of Lee's world is new, and the complexion of things is always changing.

Naomi's first grade school photo

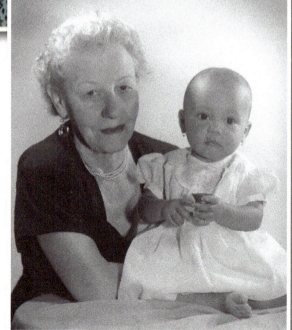

With Nanny 1954

About to leave for piano audition at age 10

With Tassie near end of Tassie's life 1965-66

Naomi and Steven...his college fraternity prom 1970

Naomi high school graduation photo 1971

Naomi at 26

With newborn son 1984

Aunt Rosemary
late 1930s

Mother dancing 1930s

Bunny at age 4-6 1916-1918

Bunny in WWII

Bunny with Langston Hughes (right) and Thaddeus Battle (left) Spanish Civil War

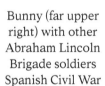

Bunny (far upper right) with other Abraham Lincoln Brigade soldiers Spanish Civil War

Parents before their marriage 1942

Mother with my son 1984

Father with my daughter 1988 and 1991

Father 1979

Mother c.2000

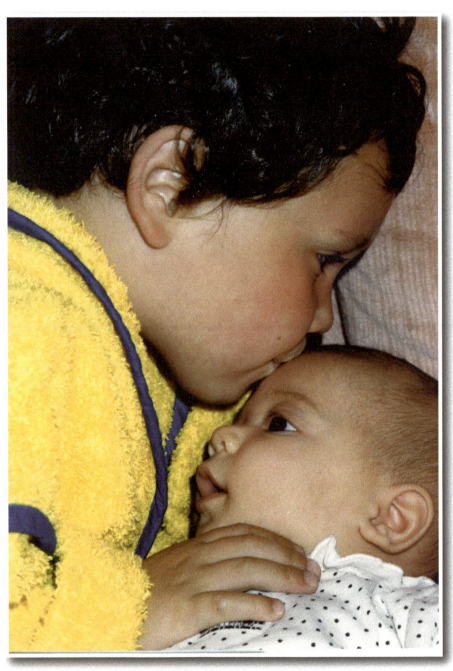

Naomi's children: Philip and Clara 1988

INTERLUDE

As we shift from recollection to commentary, a vision coalesces in my mind's eye: There is a woman, a thinker, contemplative. A young, long-haired, black-and-white dog approaches her excitedly barking. Friendly, curious, not threatening. The woman wonders what the dog is saying and where did he come from…what are the dog's thoughts? And the dog wonders what the woman might say…what are her thoughts? In the gap between the woman and the dog's mental lives lies a need for connection, a stepping-out from self-absorption.

There is recollection, memoir, that has been lived by one individual. There is theory, commentary to broaden that memoir that is yet unarticulated and exists only as thought, detached from the recollection. Our role as authors now is to find a sweet spot between them, a balancing point of connection, communication, and richer understanding between the life lived and the thoughts thought. So now we turn to theory and commentary to expand and illuminate remembrance, allowing remembrance to clarify theoretical formulation. The goal is to be reflective, not overly esoteric or intellectual, but not locked in by the immediacy of one mind's memories.

The woman smiles at the dog, and the dog quiets and sits expectantly at her feet. They begin.

INTRODUCTION TO PART TWO
Karen Lombardi, Ph.D.

Psychoanalytic theory is one of the many ways that Naomi and I are joined together. In one voice and in dual voices, we have written previously of our clinical work and of the varying theories within psychoanalysis that helped us think our thoughts. My interest in psychoanalysis is at least two-fold. Psychoanalytic theory, particularly of the neo-Kleinian and object-relations sort, has guided my clinical work with patients, my teaching of doctoral students, and my supervision of other professionals. But psychoanalysis is not simply a technique of treatment or a means of assessing unconscious processes within an individual. It is also a means of understanding groups and of the unconscious functioning of the larger culture. The aspects of theory to which I am most drawn are applicable to problems of cultural alienation and social justice. I would credit here the works of Jean-Paul Sartre, Erich Fromm, and Franz Fanon among others who have influenced me.

Here, I begin with notions of the Other embedded in both philosophy and psychoanalysis. The Other captures for me the ways in which racism, classism, sexism, and other forms of Othering are promulgated and maintained in culture. After some exploration of broader reaches of concepts of the Other, I will shift to address their implications for more individual and personal experience, such as reflected in the primary personages in Naomi's life and memoir. Our journey will move from theory to interpretation, culminating with the idea that two heads are sometimes better than one, but one head can hold two minds if the unconscious is heard.

PART TWO

THEORY, INTERPRETATION, AND A MEETING OF THE MINDS

I

THE OTHER AND THE OTHER IN US

Hegel may be accredited with the notion of the Other as it entered 19th-century philosophical discourse. The Hegelian notion of Self is dependent on, and constituted by, the existence of the Other—in this sense a facet of self-consciousness and self-reflection. Recognition by the Other is the basis of consciousness of the Self. A failure of recognition, such as seen in debasement, erasure, and the like, interferes with and constitutes a diminution of the ability to value the self and others, a "damage to self-respect" as Verhaeghe has written. We may relate this recognition of the Other in Freud's concept of negation ("this is not me") and to Spitz's concept of the child's acquisition of the capacity to voice yes and no, where the ability to distinguish between Self and Other relies on the negative.

Although not always recognized for her contribution, Simone de Beauvoir was the first to use the term "Other" regarding power relations in patriarchal culture. For her, woman was the Other, the Object, and man was the Self, the Subject, leaving the woman in the position of submission in relation to male dominance. Hers is a feminist rereading of Hegel's master-slave dialectic, in which the terms masculine and feminine are not symmetrical. Man occupies both the positive and the neutral, or the family position (as in "family of man"), while woman occupies only the negative position of the Other, the object and not the subject, the one who lacks. She quotes Aristotle: "The female is a female by virtue of a certain *lack* of qualities…we should regard the female nature as afflicted with a natural defectiveness (1952, xviii)."

Partly because of de Beauvoir's contribution, contemporary usage is no longer limited to philosophy but has entered into the common language. Othering is recognized as a mechanism whereby, through negative identifications, we relegate others who we regard as not like us, to a less-than-human status. This permits US the right to dominate, disgrace, or otherwise erase THEM. We can see the process of Othering at work in gender relations, racism, colorism, post-colonial oppression, and in all forms of difference wherein we desire to occupy positions of dominance over others to affirm ourselves and secure our own, often fantasied, sense of worth and deservedness.

From a psychoanalytic perspective, we may regard Othering as a form of projective identification, in which unwanted or dissociated parts of ourselves are projected into (attributed to) other individuals or groups. Melanie Klein speaks of projective identification as an early mode of experience wherein affects that are experienced internally are managed through projection into the (m)other. Transforming Freud's inner instinctual drives of sex and aggression into object-related passions of love and hate, she describes early, pre-verbal experiences of relationships as loving (as in soothing, satisfying, comforting) or persecutory (as in depriving, uncomfortable, restless, frustrating). We tend to split these experiences of love and hate into what Klein calls "part-object experiences," and they tend to feel all-encompassing in the moment.

Imagine, for a bit, an infant visually exploring the world with the limited visual range of early infancy. In very early infancy, the first few days or weeks of life, the infant's visual field during feeding is obscured by the breast or bottle, which comes to be experienced as either good or bad, depending upon the quality of the feeding experience. This is the first division in psychological experience. Likewise, the mother's face, eyes, arms, hair are seen in parts, which can carry good or bad affects depending upon the quality of their connection with the infant. Only later, as the infant becomes more mobile and the visual field widens, does the mother as a whole person with connected parts come into view.

Similarly, emotional bits momentarily can occupy the entire field of experience, leaving aside other bits. This is the first division in emotional (psychic) experience. The detachment of certain feelings from others constitutes splitting of experience, which protects good experiences and the good and loving object or Other from the persecutory ones. This state of splitting, Klein terms the paranoid-schizoid position. Later, sometime between the sixth and ninth month, the baby begins to integrate good and bad experience within the newfound awareness of the mother as a whole person. There is a dawning recognition that the one I momentarily hate is also the one that I ordinarily love. This same whole person can make me feel good or bad. Conversely, I am the same person who feels loving and hating, loved and hated. This mode of experience, which integrates dichotomous emotions, defines "whole-object relating." Klein calls this the depressive position, which ushers in the rudiments of guilt, responsibility, and empathy for others.

As adults, we may resort to splitting experience in the paranoid-schizoid mode when we feel consciously or unconsciously threatened or when our empathic capacities fail us. We then revert to states of projective identification in which thoughts and feelings that we cannot contain within ourselves are projected (cast into) an Other. These projected emotional experiences are then perceived as emanating from the Other, beyond our control, and therefore potentially dangerous (the paranoid element), creating anxiety that causes us to withdraw (the schizoid element).

Kristeva speaks of subjectivity as founded on Otherness—the reflection, for example, of seeing ourselves through the eyes of another. Like Klein, she posits the origin of subjectivity in early infancy, through what she calls the semiotic, the emotional realm of prelinguistic subjectivity, the capacity to experience our feelings before or without words. She describes the semiotic as a precursory sign based on Plato's chora, which for her denotes a primary sort of rhythm that precedes spatiality and temporality, a rhythm without a definite form, constituted of an early holding, pacing, and matching of rhythm in early dyadic relationships. At the same time, there is a confrontation between this (comm)union with the Other, and a radical separation or rupture, a space of difference or alienation. This process she calls abjection, akin to what Klein would refer to as the split-off parts of our psyches.

Originating in the embodied relationship between the infant and the (m) other, the processes of union and abjection, which constitute our subjectivity, continue throughout our lives and are affected by the cultures in which we reside. Subjectivity is not static, as the subject is always in process. The abjected parts of ourselves, which in Klein's terms we project onto the other, Kristeva calls "strangers to ourselves." When we encounter difference and react with fear and horror, we are enacting those abjected parts of ourselves, seemingly ridding ourselves of what we cannot tolerate, in a form of self-estrangement.

Living with social difference requires a self-reflection that recognizes that a hatred of others is a hatred of parts of ourselves. Embracing the other is an act of recognizing and embracing the Other in ourselves.

We extend this notion of the Other through Matte-Blanco's conceptualization of psychic reality as consisting of two modes of thinking and being, which he calls symmetrical and asymmetrical. To simplify, psychic life is characterized by a dynamic interaction between two fundamental types of being that exist within all of us: sameness or a lack of difference in the symmetrical mode, and difference, separation, or distinction in the asymmetrical mode. When stated in object-relational terms, the symmetrical mode represents the fundamental unity of subject and object, whereas the asymmetrical mode represents difference, distinction from others, and individuality. In symmetry, we are all human beings, we are all the same. In asymmetry, I am not you, but me. This capacity for distinction allows us to categorize our thoughts and experience, but may also lead to psychic splitting of experience, a projection of the parts of ourselves that threaten or shame us, into the Other. I am good and you are bad; I am human and you are non-human. The over-reliance on asymmetrical modes of being, as in the psychic splitting of good-me and bad-me and the projection of the bad-me into the other, leads to irrational forms of hating and Othering.

Irrational forms of hating and Othering seem to be present in most contemporary cultures. Race and class are among the major divisions that have been created to separate Self from Other. Other significant divisions include gender relations, religion, colonial oppression, and all forms of difference wherein one desires to occupy positions of dominance over others to affirm oneself and secure a sense of worth and privilege. We relegate others who are not like us to a lesser, and sometimes less-than-human, status in which we feel the right to dominate, disgrace, demean, or erase them. In doing so, we privilege difference over similarity (Dalal), and fail to recognize Sullivan's principle that we are all more simply human than otherwise.

The United States has a particularly notable history of Othering where race is concerned. The separation of the human and the non-human was codified in Article One of the United States Constitution, which declared that non-free persons shall count as three-fifths of an individual for purposes of voter representation. Non-free persons, largely Black and owned by slaveholders, were reduced to less-than-human status. This history, and its attendant consequences in the Jim Crow laws that supplemented this less-than-human status once Article One Section Two was overridden, is what I believe James "Bunny" Rucker was protesting when he entered "Human" on forms that required a box to be checked under Race. Reverberations of this history continue in policies and attitudes toward minorities, including indigenous peoples, immigrants, women, and the economically disadvantaged. I use the term "minority" advisedly, as women and the economically insecure are, at the very least (by the numbers, although not in terms of power) in the majority.

II

NAOMI'S FATHER: JAMES BERNARD RUCKER

I did have occasion to meet Naomi's mother, but I have never met her father, although I very much desired to do so. I heard snippets of his life that Naomi shared with me over the years, and I felt connected to him on that basis. I did meet one of his Abraham Lincoln Brigade colleagues, Steve Nelson, to whom I was introduced by my artist friend, Mary Fassett, during my yearly summer vacations in Truro on Cape Cod, where Nelson had retired. Nelson had co-written a book, entitled *Steve Nelson: American Radical*, which he gave to me. At that time, because of my own political interests, I was very much admiring of the Abraham Lincoln Brigade and its fight against international fascism. Knowing about Naomi's father intersected with those interests—I admired him from afar.

The Abraham Lincoln Brigade was the United States' contingent of the volunteer forces from many parts of the world who formed the International Brigades that aimed to defeat fascism in its war against the Second Spanish Republic in Spain. This conflict between fascist forces and the elected government of Spain is known as the Spanish Civil War and spanned 1936-1939. The Tamiment Library of New York University in Manhattan houses the Abraham Lincoln Brigade Archives, which contains thousands of letters written during the Spanish Civil War and the United States' subsequent entry into WWII from Brigade members to their families and friends.

Naomi's mother contributed all of Bunny Rucker's letters to the library, several of which appear in print in *The Good Fight Continues: World War II Letters from the Abraham Lincoln Brigade*. Taken together, these letters reveal the anticipatory antifascism of the Brigadiers, a volunteer group of around 2800 men and women who fought against fascism in the Spanish Civil War in the years before the full development of World War II. They presciently saw Spain as the first battleground of the ambition of fascist domination of the world. These letters also reveal the ways in which Brigadiers were stigmatized by the United States' government and the particular racism and dehumanization that they experienced in the United States in comparison to Europe.

In 1937, Langston Hughes, the noted black American journalist, poet, and author, traveled to Spain to cover the Spanish Civil War as a member of the war correspondents' fraternity. There he met other visitors from the war correspondents' fraternity, including Lillian Hellman, Dorothy Parker, Ernest Hemingway, as well as rejoining Louise Thompson, a friend and social activist of the Harlem Renaissance. One of the reasons that he went to Spain he wrote, was, "I knew that Spain once belonged to the Moors—a colored people ranging from light dark to dark white. Now the Moors have come again to Spain with the fascist armies as cannon fodder for Franco. But on the Loyalist side [the anti-fascists], there are many Negroes of various nationalities in the International Brigades. I want to write about both Moors and Negroes." (Rampersad, 2002, p. 349).

One of Hughes's first interviews was with Bunny Rucker, who became his driver and who lent him a coat of his own as Hughes had arrived without winter clothing and stayed in Spain much longer than he anticipated. A photograph of Hughes and Rucker standing next to each other, engaged in conversation with Thaddeus Battle with broad smiles on their faces can be found in Rampersad's *The Life of Langston Hughes v. 1* and is presented in this book in our selection of photos. Bunny later drove Langston to the front during the Siege of Madrid so that Hughes could report and broadcast from the front. "Here in Spain," Langston reported, "there was no prejudice; in fact, many Spanish would be considered colored in the United States. Contrary to racist American customs and expectations, blacks commanded white troops without question, and fought with skill and courage" (Rampersad, 2002, p. 350). Found among Bunny's possessions after he died by his wife, Helen, was a poem sent to him by Hughes in March 1941, which spoke to American racism and which I reproduce here:

Airplane Factories
by Langston Hughes

I see by the papers
Where the airplane factories still
Don't give no work to colored people
And it looks like they never will.
Yet it seems slightly funny -
Though I don't mean <u>funny</u> to laugh
That they don't let no colored folks
Work in defense aircraft.
They let naturalized foreigners
And some without papers
Work anywhere they want to -
Yet they start to cutting capers
If Negroes apply for jobs.
They say they're sabotaging defense
Where we ask for equal rights and try
To get down off Jim Crow's fence.
I don't understand it cause
Why on earth then, Mr. Roosevelt
Don't you give some to me?
Huh?

In their writings, both Bunny Rucker and Langston Hughes expressed the observation that their experiences of the racism within the United States far outdid the racism they experienced in other countries. Retiring to the United States from living for a time in Mexico, where his father had immigrated, Hughes re-encountered the racism that he temporarily escaped while in Mexico. Once again called "nigger," and having a restaurant worker refuse to serve him, he said: "I knew I was home in the U.S.A." (Rampersad, p.35).

African-Americans in the Abraham Lincoln Brigade, including Bunny Rucker, had similar experiences of escaping Jim Crow and experiencing themselves as human beings, not marginalized, in Spain. To quote Tom Paine, a black New Yorker, "Spain was the first place that I ever felt like a free man. If someone didn't like you, they told you to your face. It had nothing to do with the color of your skin" (Carroll et al, 2006, p. 116). And Southern-born Crawford Morgan said, "People didn't look at me with hatred in their eyes because I was black, and I wasn't refused this or refused that because I was black. I was treated like all the rest of the people were treated, and when you have been in the world for quite a long time and have been treated worse than people treat their dogs, it is quite a nice feeling to go someplace and feel like a human being" (ibid., p. 116).

As the letters collected in the archives of the Abraham Lincoln Brigade reflect, Bunny Rucker was an unusually intelligent, analytically observant person whose writing vividly described his experiences both in the Brigade and, upon his return to the United States, as an enlistee in the United States Army, which, at last, had joined the fight against fascism. The letters collected in the Tamiment Library are those that he wrote to his wife after his participation in the Brigade, while he was fighting for the United States in World War II. They reflect on his Brigade experiences while speaking in the moment of his experience in the United States Army.

Interestingly, many who fought in the Abraham Lincoln Brigade, both black and white, were marginalized in the military once the United States entered the war against fascism. Those who were prescient, those who were committed and brave enough to try to stem the cancerous growth of fascism in Europe and the racism attendant to it, were seen as untrustworthy to continue that fight for the United States.

Bunny and others were originally relegated to noncombatant units, apparently not trusted to carry arms. Milton Wolfe recounts being shifted from his training at Fort Dix to a non-combatant unit, along with Italian-Americans, German-Americans, and other "aliens who were proven in one way or the other to have been rabidly anti-fascist for as long as they could remember… who had fought Hitler and Mussy and whatever native fascists to hand they could root out, with everything they had" (Carroll et al. p.79). Those who fought against the fascists in Spain could be trusted no more than Americans of Italian or German descent—all were Othered by the United States' government. Bunny himself, "utterly disgusted with segregation, eagerly transferred to a medical unit, if only to get to Europe. Once there, he volunteered for combat in northern Italy and Germany, where he finally got his chance to fight, but was seriously wounded in 1945" (Carroll et al, p. 120).

Bunny's letters to his wife Helen, full of love and devotion, reflect his experience of Jim Crow throughout his service in World War II. The contrast between the camaraderie of his Abraham Lincoln Brigade service in Spain with the racist politics of the United States and its armed forces bears repeating. Along with his open-eyed critique of the racist politics and attitudes in the United States, his approach is always humanistic. His desire was to change the world, not just to "get those bastards," as some of the letters from others express. On the way to his initial assignment to Fort Bragg in North Carolina, Bunny writes:

> The unpleasantness of the Jim Crow ride was offset by the obvious contrast to the purposes for which all the passengers Negro and white were traveling [which belied the] deeper kinship between all oppressed peoples. It's unbelievable and impossible that a nation can exist half-slave and half-free. It's much too obviously true today for anyone with a spark of honesty to deny it or remain complacent about any feature of Jim Crow. (Carroll et. al. p. 117-118).

From Fort Bragg, Bunny writes of his continued treatment under the ethos of Jim Crow, which relegated him to limited military service, including trash disposal. It is impossible to ignore the significance of this assignment—there are those who are "honored" with full combat training and others who are relegated to the trash, referred by the government as "limited service." Protesting his assignment to limited service, he writes, "I took personal pride that I acted on the basis of my hatred of Hitlerism at all times, and I had personal hopes that I'd be given by my own country even a limited opportunity to express that hatred through some measure of participation in our armed forces. This has been effectively denied me by my transfer…into <u>non-combatant limited service</u> on a Jim Crow basis" (Carroll et al., p. 130). He goes on to remark that this blot on American democracy fails to reduce him to non-human status, writing "…I am a human being with no less sensibilities and self-respect than any other" (op. cit., p. 131).

Eventually, Bunny was transferred to Fort Huachuca, Arizona, where he enrolled in the medics, a service arm of the military, again without the right to bear arms against the enemy. Although he felt no affinity or special capability for the medics unit, it allowed him to volunteer for overseas duty. Again, he protests Jim Crow, while indicating that government policies do not always infect individual people, nor do these policies infect his personal relationships. He writes:

> I feel very close to my Irish-Catholic buddy I spoke of, the German-American, the Greek-American, and the others…But the reactionaries are afraid even to risk letting me join those buddies that way. Their superstitions make them worry even about their "other world." They want it pure and rid of the virus of mongrelization and the "slums of the world's great cities" as we are called and are treated like now (op. cit. p.134).

In an addendum to a letter to Helen, dated June 6, 1944 (D-Day), he disagrees with her optimism about race relations in the United States: "But how in the world can I hope for a picture you presented of the American people denouncing Jim Crow as fascist?" He goes on to relate an incident of a white American soldier from Oklahoma, interviewed on a newsreel that was viewed by his unit, telling the Nazis that there is equality in America. He writes:

> The whole theater rocked with boos for 15 minutes. Does this soldier call Oklahoma Jim Crow-equality? Is that the support that Negroes will expect from a Postwar America? Will a returned Army tell us that we have equality in America? Oklahoma "equality" is certainly not a war aim of the Negro people but that is what we have (op. cit. 136).

Waiting to be shipped out, he writes to Helen, expressing both his enforced separation from her while stateside in the Army because of Jim Crow miscegenation laws in the South that prohibited their relationship, and how their loving desire for each other nevertheless unites them. He writes:

> I'm sure you don't feel about Jim Crow United States the way I feel and that you feel capable of finding some satisfaction within its limitations. I never did and never will. I have never been satisfied with all the limitations you've put up with. I will never look back on those times

with any satisfaction. For every pleasure there was an insult. For every embrace there was a kick in the ass, for every kiss I was spit on. For every step toward your house there was a step back into Hell (op. cit.137).

Bunny Rucker's legacy lives on through the Tamiment Library Collection, the books that I have cited, and through items searched on the internet. He remained politically active when he returned home, organizing for the Progressive Party, running for New York City Council on the American Party line, and eventually becoming a public librarian. One recent online posting by a person whose senior thesis was on African-Americans and antifascism in the 1930s, recalls Rucker while watching the recent white supremacist rally in Charlottesville. He cites Rucker's awareness that, despite defeating Nazi Germany, the United States had (and still has) its own version of white supremacy. Like this person, I imagine that Bunny would not be surprised by the current political situation in the United States, as well as the rise in fascism in various parts of the world. At the same time, I imagine how saddened he would be.

After I wrote this section, I had the opportunity to teach a class on psychoanalysis and film. I assigned *Pan's Labyrinth,* which is set in Spain during the Spanish Civil War. To my surprise, my students were unaware of the role played by the Spanish Civil War as a prelude to World War II, nor were they aware of the significance of the Abraham Lincoln Brigade as it represented the fight for social and political justice in this country as well as in Spain. In fact, they never had even heard of the Spanish Civil War. These are especially intelligent and mature doctoral students, and as such their ignorance is not a fault in them but rather is reflective of a cultural dissociation of history from the American social consciousness. What is not spoken out of shame, or fear of losing status, or fear of the development of a social consciousness that threatens to undermine racist capitalist structures, is either whitewashed or entirely omitted from the history books. For example, our history as oppressors and colonizers is denied or simply dissociated, and recast as a fight for freedom. To refer to Matte-Blanco, when we cannot incorporate similarity with difference, difference cannot be respected, cannot achieve equal status, as it threatens our carefully constructed identity. When we cannot incorporate similarity with difference, we become paranoid and tend to split our experience into all-good and all-bad, or tend to dissociate or deny certain aspects of reality altogether. When psychic integration fails, cultural integration becomes an impossibility.

III
NAOMI'S MOTHER: HELEN MUENICH RUCKER

I have my own impression of Naomi's mother, Helen. We met in an apartment in Manhattan at a baby shower that was given in anticipation of the arrival of Naomi's first child. I remember her elegant, erect presence as she sat in the middle of a couch, facing me, perhaps a remnant of her past as a ballet dancer with the Ballet Russe de Monte Carlo. Friendly and welcoming, I also remember her as rather reserved, almost as if she was careful not to upstage others. The dance stage was one thing, interpersonal relations another.

Unlike Bunny, whose own letters and other documents referring to him allowed me to hear some of his own voice, I can only imagine and speculate where Helen is concerned. Bunny's letters afford me some insight, Naomi's memoir more. Bear with my speculation in my attempt to give Helen a bit of her own voice.

While reading Naomi's account of her mother's early years, it seemed to me (as it did to Naomi), that Helen's sister Rosemary's injury had multiple effects, both on her and on Helen. As her own form of reparative work, Rosemary not only healed her brain, but made it invincible through mastery of musical performance and multiple Ph.D.s in such disparate fields as economics, art history, and (almost) chemistry. It seems that she could wrap her brain around anything. For Helen, the traumatic accident that her sister sustained marked her from the very beginning of her life.

Soon after her birth, people came to welcome Helen into the world, and as a consequence her two-year-old sister, unattended, fell down the stairs, sustained a severe head injury, and could well have died. Although there was no way for baby Helen to "know" this cognitively, the trauma was communicated to her through the ways in which she was held, attended to, and the feelings present through holding and attention (as well as their lack). It is difficult to believe that Naomi's grandmother did not feel guilt and responsibility for the accident. The family story, at the least, conveys how painful and taxing this episode was, requiring constant ministration to Rosemary and the need to keep her physically quiet in order to protect her growing brain from fatal injury. Rosemary's accident may have instantiated a prohibition against being center stage, to which it appears that Helen was careful to adhere in her family life.

What was communicated to Helen, both consciously and unconsciously, was that there was little room for her demands, and further that she must participate in keeping quiet to aid in her sister's healing. After all, if you (Helen) demand attention or care, if you are center stage, terrible accidents can happen to others. Nevertheless, Helen became comfortable in taking the stage in her professional dancing life, which may also have a connection to her early experience. Her dancing may connect to Rosemary's accident and to early childhood prohibitions against running, jumping, or playing, as Naomi reports. Once the prohibition against movement was lifted, Helen used her body to express herself. Dance did not require making demands of others, affording her a way of enlivening herself.

Bunny's letters to Helen confirm her tendency to an unrealistic optimism regarding Jim Crow and a denial of the problems and pain of racism in the United States. This denial may be viewed as necessary to the maintenance of their relationship. Helen was not entirely color-blind as she reportedly maintained political activism against racism and other injustices in society. However, as a privileged white woman, she was in some ways immune to the racialized attacks suffered not only by her husband but by her daughter. Recognizing the problematics of difference may have threatened the identifications that she felt with her black husband and biracial daughter, identifications that held off the actual reality of being a child from a mixed marriage.

It seems that Helen's color-blindness functioned to insulate herself from the experience of her own privilege by extending that privilege to people and places where it did not exist. Helen side-stepped her own feelings of guilt for her role in bearing and raising a daughter who was subject to the vicissitudes of racism and colorism. As attentive as she was to issues of social injustice in the larger society, she was not able to apply these concerns to her own family. Helen's minimization of difference may have been an adaptive mechanism that served to join her with her husband but seemed to lead to blind spots with Naomi, as she failed to recognize her daughter's often painful reality as the child of an interracial marriage.

IV

NAOMI GABRELLA RUCKER

This section follows the chronological flow of Naomi's history, which begins with early memories. In psychoanalysis, early memories are often used as a projective technique, indicating the content of unconscious processes that mark our earliest, sometimes pre-verbal, lives. Cognitive psychologists, and some ego psychologists, opposed this psychoanalytic insight, holding that language is required for memory, and that early memories do not exist before age three or four. Recent empirical research confirms the psychoanalytic position, demonstrating that people have memories from as early as two years of age, if not before. It is my observation that these very early memories tend to be visual, not verbal, encoded in the body and the emotions, not necessarily in language. In psychoanalysis, early memories may be analyzed in ways similar to dreams, that is, as symbolic, condensed creations that speak to our hopes and desires, as well as to the traumatic experiences encoded in our embodied minds. Early memories, while factual, hold the unconscious reality of our psychic lives, representing the imprint of the relationship between our earliest experiences and their later unfoldment.

Naomi's early memories represent her capacity for pleasure and contentment, a positive sense of being held, although at a distance and from behind, as she is being pushed in a stroller. At the same time, pleasure is only partial, perhaps a bit depriving, failing to recognize Naomi's desires. Her mother allows her only a little bit of her favorite doughnut, reserving the rest and putting it out of her reach. This partial presence, this partial nurturance and subsequent deprivation and lack of recognition, leads to a rush of emotion and a precocious commitment to personal autonomy and independence. "If you won't give it to me, I will get it myself!" I do wonder, in the stroller memory, whether it is her maternal grandmother pushing her from behind, perhaps a metaphor for "having her back." If so, this memory prefigures and symbolizes the safety and pleasure she felt with her Nanny. After writing this commentary, Naomi confirmed that it was, in fact, her grandmother pushing that stroller.

Naomi's third memory is in black and white, which marks her struggle with racialization from at least age three or four. Her black and white roller coaster life is moving a bit too fast. Is it safe? Can her father catch her, keep her from danger? Here, I wonder whether Naomi is also internalizing her father's own concern and anxieties about keeping her safe as a child with interracial parents.

Repetitive childhood dreams have a particular place in psychoanalysis, sometimes representing early trauma that is unconsciously re-experienced and reworked through the dream, sometimes referring to a part of our experience that is particularly central to our being but not yet integrated into a conscious sense of ourselves. Often accompanied by feelings of anxiety or danger, we may view repetitive dreams as a kind of haunting. In Naomi's repetitive dream, which she has from ages four through twelve, and again briefly at twenty-four, a young figure who looks much like a "photo" of Naomi, wearing blue overalls, neither quite male nor quite female, stands silently, aloof and watchful. The feeling in the dream is that something bad or dangerous is about to happen, at the same time that the danger never quite materializes. There is a sense of searching for or anticipating a helpful figure who serves as a protection from danger, but this protection also fails to materialize.

The child in blue overalls seems to represent a doppelgänger, Naomi but not quite Naomi, a "photo" or a ghost of herself. This doubling is often referred to as an alter-ego, but I prefer to think of it as an encounter with the Other within the Self, a disjunction in one's subjectivity. In this sense, the doppelgänger is related to Freud's notion of the uncanny, when the unfamiliar (what is unconscious) interrupts the familiar (what is conscious), creating an encounter with unconscious parts of ourselves. This doubling occupies a particular place in the experience of race in America, as expressed in DuBois's concept of double consciousness, the sometimes simultaneous and sometimes split experience of one's self contrasted with one's awareness of how one is seen by others. In the recent novel, *The Love Songs of W.E.B. DuBois,* the main character, Ailey Pearl Garfield, has a doppelgänger in the form of a long-haired woman who appears in moments of stress. Her ghostly presence serves as a form of protection, a desired part of Ailey that simultaneously alerts her to danger and serves as a reminder of the internal strength that keeps her going.

In Naomi's dream of the toddler resembling herself, wearing blue overalls, she is the often-sad-overall child, both girl and boy, both her mother and her father, always observant but perhaps too silent. In her dreams, the overall child appears as a reminder of her doubling, her split consciousness, at the same time the dream figure disappears when the mood gets too anxious or dangerous. It seems, from Naomi's associations, that the anxiety contained in this repetitive dream was related both to her mother's tendency to evaporate and the tenuous experience, appearing and disappearing, of her father's playfulness. In the recent iteration of this dream that Naomi had while finishing this book, returning to hold the toddler symbolizes a move toward psychic wholeness as she gathers together the split-off emotional pieces represented by her doppelgänger. Now she can hold herself.

Holding is a theme that recurs throughout Naomi's psychohistory. As previously mentioned, holding is a concept developed by Winnicott and taken up in various ways by Stern, Beebe, and Kristeva. They draw attention to the critical nature of holding, breathing patterns, and the matching of body rhythms in the early infant-caregiver dyad in the development of intersubjectivity, reinforcing or interrupting experiences of unity and disunity, similarity and difference. Naomi recounts the story of her family dog, Tassie, her friend and confidante, being held continuously by Nanny throughout a bout of pneumonia when she was a puppy, saving her life. We might see this as a metaphor for Naomi's relationship with Nanny, whom she experienced as providing life-saving safety and security. Naomi recounts being wrapped under Nanny's arm in her big fur coat, protecting her from cold winds, testifying to the loving warmth that she felt with her grandmother. She also describes her father's warm embrace as providing a sense of comfort and security.

Parents not only provide a holding environment for their children as a receptive or passive activity; it is critical that loving desire is a part of holding. Bunny, suffering from wartime wounds and using crutches as he anticipated his child's birth, forced himself to do without crutches, as it was important to him that he be able to hold his baby. This heroic effort is testimony to his desire to be whole, strong, and embracing for his child, which it appears Naomi felt with him throughout much of her life.

Early experiences of racism elicited a different sort of protection, both from Nanny and from Naomi's father. Naomi's memory of her arm being yanked by her grandmother was experienced with confusion: "Why is Nanny hurting me?" only to later discover that she was being protected, pulled out of the way of a racist woman who was trying to close the exterior apartment building door on Naomi. Similarly, her father physically restrained an Emergency Room physician; he falsely believed that the physician was refusing proper care to Naomi when she was injured because of her color. Holding and the provision of safety are not simply receptive functions; sometimes they require strong actions and interventions.

These anecdotes are reminders of the misunderstanding by our culture of the interventions some parents are moved to make in the impulse to protect their children. Protection requires action but is often misunderstood. In recent news coverage, a mother was criticized and accused of abuse for giving a slap to her son's head because she feared for his life during a George Floyd demonstration. This misunderstanding—that this is parental abuse and not a gesture of parental protection—that we don't hit or grab our children—is a color-blind form of denial, ignoring the dangers of being black (or the Other of any other color) in a white society.

To continue to speak of Naomi's relationship with her family, and particularly her relationship with her mother, I will reenter psychoanalytic theory through the psychological world of the infant. This time my focus is on the development of the Self in relation to the Other, rather than primarily on the problematics of Otherness. Unlike Freudian theory, which views the infant as a closed system dominated by biological drives of sex and aggression, only gradually incorporating others as the ego develops, both Naomi and I share an object-relations perspective, which attributes relatedness with others from the beginning of life.

Mental and psychological experience, at least from birth, are primary in the theoretical formulations of Melanie Klein. She departs from Freudian theory, distinguishing between Self and Other as occurring through the psychological mechanisms of projection and introjection, rather than the internal working of biological instincts that Freud theorized. Further, she translated Freud's biological instincts of sex and aggression into human emotions of love and hate. From a Kleinian perspective, we attempt to rid ourselves of unpleasant, undesired, hateful parts of our experience by projecting them onto others. Similarly, we absorb desired and loving qualities of others into ourselves. We are then psychologically linked to others through identification, the partner of introjection, and unlinked to others through dis-identification, the partner of projection. "I am like you, you are like me" is counterposed with "I am not like you, you are not like me." "We" is a statement of mutual introjection and identification, whereas "Them" is a statement of projection and dis-identification.

These processes are unconscious, not deliberate, sometimes subtle, sometimes less subtle, but they are always occurring in our relationships with individuals as well as with groups. Introjection and projection are present at birth, developing in tandem with nurturance and deprivation. Both Naomi and I believe that this process begins before birth, in the mind and feelings of the (m)other (including the father or other partner) as phantasies, feelings, and concerns about the coming child. The particular spelling of "phantasy" in the Kleinian framework refers to unconscious thoughts and feelings that exist from the beginning of life as opposed to the conscious imaginings suggested by "fantasy." Conscious expectations are outwardly detectable, cognitively mediated, and verbally coded. But the affective states with the most psychological impact on the baby may be those that are unconscious or unacknowledged, forming a template for the early (m)other-baby relationship.

Klein speaks of projection as a very early mode of experience and relating, in which painful internal emotions are discharged (externalized) by the baby and contained by the (m)other (nurturing figure), and then experienced as originating in the (m)other, not in the self. These affects are managed by the (m)other who, under favorable circumstances, contains, tames, and modulates them, creating projective-introjective cycles, wherein the baby, in turn, takes in (introjects) the mother's soothing. If the projected affects fail to be contained and managed by the other, they carry a dangerous potential to disrupt the infant, as negative emotions that have failed to be modulated, remain alien, and are potentially disorganizing. The infant withdraws in anxiety, which can disrupt a sense of loving holding, if it is excessive or chronic.

This process is known by Klein to be the paranoid-schizoid position, paranoid referring to fear of what is externally threatening, and schizoid referring to withdrawal. The paranoid-schizoid position is expressed in relation to an object (person), by which Klein refers to aspects of the (m)other, and is a normal development in the first months of life. It can be present or reemerge throughout one's psychological life under specific circumstances, hence the term "position," rather than "phase" or "stage." The hallmark of the paranoid-schizoid position is the origination of splitting, a psychic defense by which emotional experience is divided (split) into all-good and all-bad, creating a rudimentary separation of Self and Other.

Through projective identification, the person projects feelings from the Self into the Other, who receives the projection and ideally returns the feelings in modified, soothing, loving form. When persecutory (bad) feelings are returned unmodified, perhaps because the (m)other is too anxious, too stressed, too full of her own persecutory feelings, or simply fails to attend, the paranoid-schizoid position is reinforced. The paranoid-schizoid dynamic is the root of both idealization of self and others, and denigration and related phenomena, such as prejudice, phobias, and sado-masochism. It also is central to relational problems in families and groups, including envy, destructive competitiveness, and repetitive patterns of domestic abuse.

Although the overall context of Naomi's infancy and early childhood was loving and attentive, absent gross neglect or abuse, there are indications of a lack of recognition on the part of her mother that can be discerned in her narrative. This lack prefigures her birth, with her mother's lack of awareness of her pregnancy until the fourth month of gestation. As Naomi recounts, her mother's water broke some days before her contractions began. Once she began to experience contractions, she insisted they were gas pains. It was only when Naomi's father insisted that she was in labor that she agreed to go to the hospital. In Naomi's sense of her prenatal experience, there was no recognition by her mother that a new being was growing, that something other than Helen's own Self existed. Was there room for another?

The failure to make sufficient room for a baby, the failure to acknowledge pressing needs (including the failure to recognize the physically pressing need to be born), became integral to Naomi's later difficulties with a sense of being loved and lovable, important in her mother's world, and, perhaps most significantly, with the sense of not being seen. It is further remarkable that Naomi's memoir includes many examples of embodied relationships with Nanny and Bunny, including the warmth and safety of being held; the comfort of an embodied relationship appears infrequent or absent with her mother. This embodied connection did, however, express itself symbolically, though at a distance; Naomi's interest in modern dance, and later horseback riding, expresses some of this connection with her mother absent a direct connection.

Naomi's love for English riding is associated with her mother's race and class privilege. Perhaps, more importantly, the attunement of bodily connection between the horse and the rider provided an experience that was partially lacking and longed-for in Naomi's physical relationship with her mother. Her joy in riding was the experience of being "in the zone" where the horse and rider are in bodily synchrony. Jumping fences and obstacles, which added an element of danger, was especially satisfying—rising in the air, landing on the other side, remaining connected, moving forward. She could cross the abyss and reach solid ground on the other side.

Naomi speaks of feeling "tainted," which appears to be connected to the early difficulties with an intimate embodied relationship with her mother, but also to her mother's denial about racial matters. Naomi's struggles with her biracial heritage, which left her with a sense that she fit neither in the "black world" nor the "white world," may have been inevitable growing up in the United States in the 1950s-1960s. Even if this is so, however, this circumstance was complicated by her mother's inability to recognize or speak of racial difference, again, a form of denial. In Naomi's words, "For my mother, especially, a person's color was totally unimportant, and she lived by this creed." Naomi was left on her own to struggle with issues of identity. Her sense of being tainted may be seen as a reflection of her mother's unconscious feelings of carrying a biracial child. Taint implies a distorted, darkening color, a blot, with obvious meaning in the context of an interracial family. (As a note, I use the term "interracial" advisedly, as Bunny's own family was multi-racial. However, in our culture, the one-drop rule still seems to apply.)

In terms of Naomi's personal history, "taint" also seems to imply the debasement and disowning of the qualities of the baby to come, a dis-identification, a need to create psychological distance from the pregnancy and the fetus. Naomi may have entered this world holding emotions of being tainted and rejected that originated unconsciously in her mother, coexisting alongside being a longed-for and cherished child. Her early weeks of crying and her mother's inability to soothe her likely reflected and compounded this problem. Comfort from her father and Nanny was available, as they did not seem to carry the same unconscious affects about Naomi's racial self. Closeness with them was consoling, but closeness with her mother was laced with tension.

Helen's tendency to "evaporate" or emotionally disappear was paralleled by her physical presence, followed by her absence, as she returned to her full-time job three weeks after Naomi's birth. The five weeks of crying as a neonate and then apparently giving up that the memoir describes was replayed in Naomi's life as she struggled with depression and withdrawal as a child, withdrawing again socially in early adulthood, and eventually giving up hope. The theme, not of debasement, per se, but of distance and absence propelled by debasement, marked Naomi's relationship with her mother and would be reactivated in other aspects of her interpersonal life. Her comment to me about her experiences of relatedness with others is that she is comfortable with connection and intimacy but has difficulty tolerating absence. Winnicott speaks about capacity to generate a sense of presence in absence—that is, when the other is physically absent, there remains a sense of psychic presence, a sense of confidence, internalization of the other, that assures the survival of relatedness. With her mother, this sense of "presence in absence," a confidence that the other would return was deficient.

Many origins relevant to Naomi's deep-seated sense of being "inadequate," "defective," or "tainted" can be traced to the dynamics of the paranoid-schizoid and depressive positions. Naomi felt that she was inadequate in maintaining a connection with her mother, and her mother may have felt similarly. Her father had psychological and physical inadequacies that Naomi may have absorbed and taken in as her own. Nanny was her rescuer, her savior, the person to whom she would go to escape negatively-toned projections and feelings in order to feel protected and immersed in good.

Nanny was probably the most integrated of the family trio of parenting figures. Bunny had access to good and bad feelings about race and other things and could express ambivalence, empathy, and remorse, but alcohol intermittently derailed his integrative capacities. When he was drinking, his rage and hurt dominated. Helen was a well-integrated woman, particularly in her work life, while at the same time suffering from an absence-in-presence in relation to Naomi, as well as a denial of racial differences, which affected Naomi negatively. Nanny was the one most able to contain Naomi's feelings in a steady, consistent manner without needing to dissociate or repress affects (like Helen) or express them in extreme, disorganized ways (like Bunny).

Aspects of the mothering that Naomi received seem to have expressed intermingled qualities of both the paranoid-schizoid and the depressive positions. Ambivalence, a depressive position feature, is evident, but so are dissociated aspects of the Self and Other that are paranoid-schizoid markers. Naomi's mother's disowned, unconscious emotions around "blackness" seemed to have been present from the beginning of her pregnancy onward, neither truly acknowledged nor recognized by her mother during her pregnancy, nor during Naomi's childhood. As Naomi observed, Helen was oblivious to racial distinctions. Her denial of racial tensions in her daughter's life may have had roots in a concomitant denial of the implications of marrying a black man and having his child. As Naomi comments, marrying a black man was one thing, but having a child with him was another. Naomi did not doubt Helen's devotion to Bunny, but at times she felt herself to be an unwanted intruder to her mother and to her mother's bond with her father.

I imagine a paradox here; race can be erased if it belongs to another, but not if it belongs, through bearing a biracial child, to oneself. If so, this is evidence of Helen's splitting when it came to her relationship to her daughter. The inability to acknowledge racial issues with her daughter suggests dissociated (split-off) guilt for harming her daughter and for the racism that she could not face. Her ability to conceive only after believing that her husband was sterile suggests an unconscious emotional factor in their years of infertility related to disowned negatively-toned feelings.

The Kleinian formation of the depressive position also can be seen through Naomi's struggle to resist falling into a paranoid-schizoid mode. Her lifelong depressive urges, punctuated by withdrawal and intermittent suicidal thoughts, ordinarily are seen as a failure of the depressive position. However, this struggle also reflected some capacity to bring together the loving and hating feelings within herself and her parents, no matter how painful they may be. As frightful as they may seem, fantasies of throwing herself into an abyss or into the ocean may represent a loving desire for unity, a desire to reach her mother on the other side of the emotional gulf between them. At the same time, these fantasies reflect a self-loathing connected with feelings of defectiveness and taint. Resisting these urges and restraining herself represent a desire for self-preservation, and by extension, love of self. Taken together, these two poles, the positive and negative, the loving and the self-loathing, reflect her struggles to tolerate the ambivalence of the depressive position.

It is perhaps not uncommon to very much want a pregnancy and a child, and, simultaneously, not to want one. Feelings of ambivalence during pregnancy, including anxiety and doubt, while consciously expressed by many, are likely unconsciously experienced by many more. Naomi felt both loved and hurt by her mother, desired and unwanted or unrecognized from her very inception/conception. Part of this lack of recognition seemed related to Helen's own difficulties facing her own phantasies, feelings, and actions as they were too disruptive and disorganizing to her own sense of self. Some of Helen's feelings needed to be split-off, kept from her awareness, in order to sustain her identity as someone for whom race does not matter. It is possible that her negative feelings about bearing a mixed-race baby were, themselves, cast-off feelings toward her husband that she did not permit herself to experience so as not to trouble her marriage or her view of it. The only way to unite her good and bad feelings was to deny the difference of race.

Naomi felt her denial of difference. Helen may not have felt ambivalent about her pregnancy on a conscious level, but her unconscious feelings about having a mixed-race child were conveyed to Naomi if only through Helen's inability to notice and speak of the ways in which racialization affected her. For Naomi, who absorbed these disowned feelings so early in her existence, being "tainted" became an organizing aspect of her self. It is important to note that Naomi was not "tainted" by her genetics but by Helen's unconscious projections that were internalized by her.

As Helen could not allow ambivalent feelings in herself around issues of race, she was not able to be receptive to her child's struggles and help her process them safely. Race became a split-off aspect of their relationship, one that Naomi and Helen could not openly discuss together. Helen's marriage was racially integrated, but her own internal integration around race eluded her. As Naomi's father underscores in a letter to his wife (see my earlier discussion), Helen saw race relations through "rose-colored glasses," believing in a post-racial society and failing to recognize her husband's pain and anger around the ways in which Jim Crow affected their relationship. As she did with her husband, so she later did with her daughter.

To return to Matte Blanco, our psychic reality operates simultaneously in symmetrical and asymmetrical modes. Symmetry occupies the space of similarity, an undifferentiated mode of experience wherein all is the same. Asymmetry occupies the space of difference and differentiation, wherein we are able to make distinctions; herein resides the sense of individuality. Dalal employs Matte Blanco's formulation to speak of the process of racialization. When we over-stress similarity, we tend to deny difference. When we over-stress difference, we tend to deny similarity. Healthy functioning acknowledges similarity within difference, and the difference within similarity, allowing for the maintenance of relationships to others without needing to erase the complexity of our identities.

Processes of racialization, and of groups in general, tend to consider only difference, separating one group from another. In the extremity, "I am not you. We share nothing in common." The problematics of Naomi's relationship with her mother tend to suggest that Helen, in over-stressing similarity, was compromised in her ability to integrate difference without threatening her psychic relationship to her daughter. Naomi, in turn, felt the denial of difference that erased or spoiled aspects of her Self and marginalized her sense of connection to her mother. She had to be like her mother, oblivious to race, to keep their connection, but she could not do so.

Naomi's father, perhaps better able to hold difference within similarity and similarity within difference, nevertheless suffered his own depression due to deprivations in his early life, the failure of his body to remain whole, and the failure of his political efforts to create a more just society. Falling into the depression of her father and suffering from the denial of her mother, she turned to herself—first as an avid reader and an excellent student, later as an accomplished professional and a competent single mother, and a sometimes, but always reluctant, participant in groups. Caught in-between, where else was there to go? She went to the unconscious, of herself and of others, from which she has both suffered and benefitted.

AFTERTHOUGHTS
Karen Lombardi

Reading this memoir brought me to my relationship with Naomi, and the similarity-in-difference and the difference-in-similarity that have joined us over the years. Naomi and I first met as classmates in our post-doctoral psychoanalytic training, where a group of sixteen of us met in weekly classes over the course of four years. I was immediately drawn to her, to her passion, her liveliness, and to her sharp intellect; when she spoke in class, I felt that her voice echoed my voice. We quickly became fast friends. I was there during her first pregnancy and the birth of her first child, and have fond remembrances of going for drives in her car, which soothed her baby son. In reading her psychohistory, I was reminded of the similarity, in relation to her own child, to her early memory of her feeling of comfort while being pushed in a stroller. Times and geography change, city strollers become suburban cars, but the communicated feeling is the same.

As we got to know each other, I discovered how much personal history we shared often on an implicit or unconscious level. I was a voracious reader as a child. Naomi is the only person I know who read more books as a child than I did, and she exceeded me by quite a bit. We each had our reasons for getting lost (and found) in books. In reading her story, I discovered other aspects we share, often on an unconscious level. We each had repetitive childhood dreams that still live in our awareness. She sleepwalked as a child at the same age that I began to sleepwalk. Her forays were perhaps more adventurous, taking her out of the house and into her neighborhood, while I wandered from floor to floor, upstairs to downstairs, within my house. Were we anxious children who needed to find others, to make sure they were there and safe, in our sleep?

Or were we moving toward a trauma that we were reliving in our sleep? All is possible.

Both only children, we each had an imaginary companion, both with a girl's name. Hers was Ethel, mine was Suki. Naomi recounts that her imaginary companion was named after a white friend of her mother, which may have served to bring her into closer loving identification with her mother. I was especially struck by the form of her father's anxiety while awaiting the birth of his child, a worry fed by his supposedly damaged sperm, that "the baby would have two heads." Naomi speculates that her sense of being defective might have paralleled her father's experience of himself and was not solely an artifact of her unconscious connection with her mother. However, I have continued to wonder about the meaning of a baby with two heads.

I had written a paper some time ago entitled, "Instead of One Head I've Got Two (and You Know Two Heads are Better Than One)." The title of the paper, an homage to a favorite bebop song of mine, addressed a film about the complex identity of a Christian Ethiopian boy airlifted to Israel to escape war in his country, living as Jew of color in white-dominated Israel. I wonder whether having "two heads" was Bunny's unconscious anxiety about bringing a biracial child into the world. And, at the same time, didn't he have two heads, a double consciousness, á la Du Bois? And sometimes might two heads be better, or at least more realistic, than one?

Music is another theme running through Naomi's life story. She speaks of the songs that her father sang to her that communicated his feelings about their relationship. Maurice Chevalier's "Thank Heaven For Little Girls" expressed his gratitude for having her as his daughter; Louis Armstrong's "Hello Dolly" expressed his pleasure at having her "right home where she belonged" and affirmed her beauty "You're looking swell, Dolly." There is a further unconscious connection here. When she was a baby, her father would call her his "Dolly Dingle," making Armstrong's song remarkably appropriate.

There were two songs, especially, that touched Naomi and made her cry. Harry Belafonte's "Kingston Town" was perhaps the most poignant. "I left a little girl in Kingston Town" evokes feelings of connection and anticipated loss with Bunny's childhood family as well as with Naomi. Naomi points out Harry Belafonte's mixed-race heritage, representing another unconscious connection. Perhaps most moving is Nat King Cole's "Walking My Baby Back Home," and these lyrics: "Gee it's great after being out late, Walking my baby back home. Arm in arm over meadow and farm, Walking my baby back home.

We go along harmonizing a song, Or I'm reciting a poem…" and so on. A reunion song of affirmation, of closeness, of connection and togetherness, of eternality, but not too sentimental, contrasts with Belafonte's song of loss and abandonment. Both are part of Bunny's story, Naomi's story, and part of all our stories of connection and loss.

Naomi goes on to speak about her own taste in music and the pressure to conceal her interest in "white" music like the Beatles and the Rolling Stones with her black friends, and to hide her love for Motown with her white friends. Her experience both unites and divides us. I, too, prefer Motown and feel it to be my music (is that presumptuous for a white girl?), but I had no need to hide my preferences. And I, as a white girl, was an avid listener of the New York City radio station WBLS. Some white folks did listen to black radio stations! I do wonder whether my comfort in crossing boundaries was an artifact of my "white privilege," (which I acknowledge culturally but do not always feel personally). Or might it also be the difference between the culture of Naomi's New Jersey neighborhood in the 60s and 70s as distinguished from my Manhattan life during that same time? All those speculations aside, as much as Naomi and I have shared, I was surprised that I had no indication until I read this memoir that Motown was another connection between us. But there you are. It lingers. Certain expressions of race are not to be spoken of. Or listened to. Or acknowledged.

What can we allow ourselves to feel, what can we allow ourselves to know, what can we allow ourselves to speak, if we are not to fall into a void? In states of extreme symmetrization, everything is everything, no thing can be separated from any other thing, and thinking is impossible. In states of extreme asymmetry, nothing is related to any other thing, our reality fragments into smaller and smaller bits, and connections are lost—they disappear. Both extremes lead us to a void. In terms of human relatedness, our task is to find ourselves in others and to recognize the other in ourselves, to accept difference without alienation and derogation, and to accept similarity without foreclosure. We may then color ourselves and others, human.

FINAL VERSE
Naomi Rucker

Following the theme of music, present in the stories of Rosemary's talent, my mother's piano-playing, my piano life, my father's favorite songs and his singing to me, and Karen's and my love of classic oldies soul music, I will share a last remembrance, a final verse. One of my father's favorite songs, one that he played on our hi-fi frequently, was Louis Armstrong's "It's a Wonderful World." To this day, that song can bring tears to my eyes. The lyrics are an ode to the simpler things in life—beauty, trees, flowers, a rainbow, sung to music that haunts. "The faces of the rainbow, so pretty in the sky, are also on the faces of people going by…" The faces of the rainbow, a reference to the range of complexions that Satchmo seemed to admire as "pretty," a beautiful aspect of humanity.

In this song, Louis Armstrong conveys a love for living and a pleasure in the wonders of the everyday world, sentiments that my father sustained despite his personal anguish and disappointments. The lyrics also convey motifs of love, nature, and babies growing, all themes that probably touched my father's heart. Even during his years of depression, Bunny would have agreed that "It's a Wonderful World." In this sentiment, he lived in symmetry with my mother, embracing idealism and hope. To me, asymmetry asserts itself. My father's life, his life with my mother, my life with both of them, and my independent life capture the pathos that exists in the human condition; they are all bittersweet.

REFERENCES

Bentall, Richard (1992). A proposal to classify happiness as a psychiatric disorder. *Journal of Medical Ethics, 18, 94-98.*

Brooks, Walter E. (1927-1958) *Freddy the Pig* series. New York: Alfred A. Knopf

Carroll, Peter M., Nash, Michael, and Small, Melvin (2006). *The Good Fight Continues: World War II Letters from the Abraham Lincoln Brigade.* New York and London: New York University Press.

Dalal, Farhad (2002). *Race, Color and the Processes of Radicalization: New Perspectives from Group Analysis, Psychoanalysis and Sociology.* London and New York: Routledge.

De Beauvoir, Simone (1952). *The Second Sex.* New York: Alfred A. Knopf.

DuBois, W.E.B. (1903/1994) *The Souls of Black Folk.* New York: Dover.

Fanon, Frantz (1952). *Black Skin, White Masks.* New York: Grove Press.

Freud, Sigmund (1900). *Interpretation of Dreams. Standard Edition, v. ix.* London: Hogarth Press.

————————(1925) *Negation. Standard Edition, v. xix,* 233-240. London: Hogarth Press.

Fromm, Erich (1941). *Escape from Freedom.* New York: Henry Holt, 1994.

Hegel, G.W.F. (187/2019). *The Phenomenology of Spirit.* Cambridge: Cambridge University Press.

Jeffers, Honoree Fanzine (2021). *The Love Songs of W.E.B. DuBois.* New York: Harper.

Klein, Melanie. *Love, Guilt and Reparation and Other Works,* 1921-1945. New York: Free Press, 1975.

Kristeva, Julia. (1991). *Strangers to Ourselves.* New York: Columbia University Press.

Lombardi, Karen (2014). Instead of One Head I've Got Two (and You Know Two Heads are Better Than One. Annual Meeting of the Association for the Psychoanalysis of Culture and Society, Rutgers University.

Matte Blanco, Ignacio (1975), *The Unconscious as Infinite Sets*. London: Duckworth.

———————— (1988). *Thinking, Feeling, and Being*. New York: Routledge.

Moi, Toril (ed.) (1986) *The Kristeva Reader*. New York: Columbia University Press

Nelson, Steve, Barrett, James R., and Ruck, Rob. (1981) *Steve Nelson, American Radical*. Pittsburgh: University of Pittsburgh Press.

Guillermo del Toro (2006). *Pan's Labyrinth*. Warner Brothers.

Rampersad, Arnold (2002). *The Life of Langston Hughes. Vol. I: 1902-1941. I, Too, Sing America*. Oxford and New York: Oxford University Press.

Remembrance 2020: The Wisconsin Bail Out the People Movement. Online Source.

Rucker, Naomi and Lombardi, Karen (1998). *Subject Relations: Unconscious Experience and Relational Psychoanalysis*. New York: Routledge.

Sartre, Jean-Paul (1943). *Being and Nothingness*. New York: Washington Square Press, 2021

Spitz, Rene (1957). *No and Yes: On the Genesis of Human Communication*. New York: International Universities Press.

Stern, Daniel (1985). *The Interpersonal World of the Infant: A View from Psychoanalysis and Developmental Psychology*. New York: Basic Books.

Sullivan, Harry Stack (1953). *The Interpersonal Theory of Psychiatry*. New York: W.W. Norton

Verhaeghe, Paul (2014). *What About Me? The Struggle for Identity in a Martlet-Based Society*. New York: Vintage.

Wilkerson, Isabel (2011). *The Warmth of Other Suns; The Epic Story of America's Great Migration*. New York: Vintage.

————————(2020) *Caste: The Origins of Our Discontents*. New York: Random House.

Winnicott, D.W. (1965). *The Maturational Process and Facilitating Environment*. London: Hogarth Press.

————————(1971). *Playing and Reality*. London and New York: Routledge.

AUTHOR BIOS

Drs. Rucker and Lombardi are psychologists/psychoanalysts with decades of experience in academia and private practice, and a long-standing friendship and professional affiliation. Dr. Rucker has taught psychoanalytic theory and clinical technique on the undergraduate, graduate, and post-graduate levels in New York, California, and currently in Georgia. During her years in Southern California, she was a Training and Supervising Analyst with two psychoanalytic institutes. Dr. Lombardi is Professor at the Derner Institute for Advanced Psychological Studies at Adelphi University, where she teaches and supervises doctoral students in clinical psychology. She has been a Teaching and Supervising Analyst in two analytic training programs, in the New York City area and the Pacific Northwest. She has published and presented clinical and scholarly material both nationally and internationally. Together they have presented and published numerous clinical and theoretical papers in psychoanalysis, including a co-authored book entitled *Subject Relations: Unconscious Experience and Relational Psychoanalysis,* published by Routledge in 1988.

Dr. Rucker also is the mother of two grown children and the grandmother of a young grandson. Her son is an internationally recognized newspaper journalist and editor and a two-time Pulitzer Prize winner. Her daughter is a successful geophysicist/geologist now working with a global engineering company. She is also the mother of the best grandchild one could ask for! Dr. Lombardi is the mother of a grown daughter, artistically talented and much beloved. She currently is a doctoral candidate in clinical psychology, committed to psychoanalytic practice and social justice. Her mother is exceedingly proud of her.

Printed in the USA
CPSIA information can be obtained
at www.ICGtesting.com
LVHW052204090524
779692LV00016B/280